The Joy of Living Salt-Free

The Joy of
Living
Salt-Free

Ralph E. Minear, M.D.

Macmillan Publishing Company
New York
Collier Macmillan Publishers
London

Macmillan Publishing Company
866 Third Avenue, New York, N.Y. 10022
Collier Macmillan Canada, Inc.

Library of Congress Cataloging in Publication Data
Minear, Ralph E.
    The joy of living salt free.
    Bibliography: p.
    Includes index.
    1. Hypertension—Diet therapy—Recipes. 2. Salt-free
diet—Recipes. 3. Hypertension—Prevention. I. Title.
RC685.H8M527   1984   616.1'320654   84-3893
ISBN 0-02-585060-1

Macmillan books are available at special discounts for bulk purchases
for sales promotions, premiums, fund-raising, or educational use. Special
editions or book excerpts can also be created to specification. For details,
contact:
    Special Sales Director
    Macmillan Publishing Company
    866 Third Avenue
    New York, New York 10022

10 9 8 7 6 5 4 3 2 1

Printed in the United States of America

To Sabina and Nicholas

Contents

ACKNOWLEDGMENTS

First, I want to thank Bill Adler for suggesting I write about my experience. Also, I am very grateful to Bruce Cassiday for organizing all of the information in a coherent manner, and to several Boston nutritionists who corrected and offered excellent additions to the manuscript and menus. Finally, I am appreciative of Patrick Filley and his staff at Macmillan for their help in editing the manuscript.

Introduction

Since an early time in my medical career I have been interested in the impact of various nutrients upon an individual's health, in part since my patients want and need advice about nutrition as it relates to their health. The importance of adequate nutrition was made very vivid to me when I was studying during the 1960s in the Caribbean and Southeast Asia. But the consequences of nutrition and health had a broader meaning for me after I had been a participant in the White House Conference on Food, Nutrition and Health in 1969.

In particular the White House Conference recommended that obesity and the use of salt as contributors to hypertension should be controlled or eliminated. Professionally this was important to me because I was then physician to many inner-city poor and improperly nourished individuals. My colleagues and I worked very hard to provide patients with a program to increase their physical fitness, control their weight, reduce their salt use and eliminate other factors thought to be contributing to hypertension.

Personally I wasn't aware of my salt intake until some ten years ago when I began to analyze the foods I had eaten so readily before. It was all part of an evaluation of my state of health, spurred on partially by the fact that the incidence of hypertension in my family is high. I was surprised at the amount of sodium in my diet. Indeed, I was not following my own advice. Excess sodium was not to be a part of my diet so I began to reduce its intake. And now that I have adapted to my low-sodium diet program, salty foods really cause my taste buds to screech.

I know it is not easy to change to a low-salt diet and even less so to maintain it. I thought my experience was important enough to share with you. The strategies for reducing the salt load in my diet, and menus for maintaining a diet relatively salt-free, have turned out to be very successful for me and a number of my friends and patients. I hope that after reading this book you will find, as I have found, the joy of living salt-free.

1

Confessions of a Salt-Hater

The truth of the matter is that I never really did like the taste of salt. I didn't even like the way it changed the flavor of foods that I did like. But in order to fit into the society of my birth, I tried to alter my natural taste to adapt to the flavors and likes of my peers.

By the time I was an adult, I was as addicted to salt and as wooed by its blandishments as anyone else. I had become a victim of the sodium mystique years before it began to be known that salt—in particular its constituent, sodium—could be a killer.

My basic instincts had been right. I was a victim of social mores and culinary convention—on the gourmet level, ironically enough.

My first encounter with the fascinating power of salt occurred when I was a very young boy. We lived in an area where fresh fruits and vegetables were available almost the year round, where food was inexpensive and easily prepared, and in a family that was not really a slave to the allure of rich seasonings or spices.

Also, my mother was a fanatic for natural food long before it ever became fashionable. She used as little flavoring as possible, preferring to serve food without artificial enhancement. We did have salt and pepper in the house, but mostly for company.

The Adventure of the Unseasoned Watermelon

It was my uncle who reached for the salt one afternoon during some special holiday, frantically shaking it over a freshly cut slice of watermelon. Since then I have watched hundreds of people do the same thing, but up to that moment, I had never seen such a strange act.

"Why are you putting salt on fresh watermelon?" I asked in wonder.

"To improve the taste," my uncle replied, astonished and eyeing me oddly.

I looked around for help. None came. My parents continued eating.

"But it tastes good *now!*" I protested.

My uncle shrugged. "Can't stand it without salt," he told me, and, to back up his statement, poured more on before he continued to spoon out the fresh fruit.

My own slice of watermelon was luscious—cool, sweet, tasty. I decided to experiment. Could it be made even more tasty? I reached for the saltshaker and tipped some on. The salt subsided into the fruit, becoming invisible. I spooned out a bite and began to chew it.

"Oh, no!" I cried and spat it out.

It was terrible-tasting. The soft, gentle, sensitive flavor of the fruit was overlaid with a vile, almost bitter flavor that reached down to my toes, ruining the sweetness of the taste I was so used to.

Immediately I was punished for disrespectful behavior at the dinner table. However, I had learned a powerful lesson. Not everyone had quite the same idea of what tasted good. As for myself, I continued to avoid salt on watermelon all through my childhood.

When I told my uncle that the salt tasted terrible on the watermelon, he simply said, "Everyone to his own taste," reinforcing my own lesson learned that afternoon.

My uncle was wrong. He was wrong in preferring the adulterated taste of salted watermelon to the pure flavor of fresh watermelon. He was also wrong in saying that it was impossible to understand or discuss taste with anybody else.

But at the time it seemed that he was right.

Soon enough, my sheltered childhood was over and I began to find myself in the company of others besides family members at meals, including sieges of institutionalized eating away at school. An odd thing began to happen. I found myself more and more unable to face what was on my plate without reaching for the saltshaker to help disguise the taste. I began to understand why friends were astounded to learn that I did not use salt and pepper on my food. And so, because I hated to be a freak, I took up seasoning with salt and pepper—with a vengeance.

I even began putting salt on watermelon and conceived the fantasy that it tasted better that way. As for the food I was served in restaurants, I knew from immediate experience that it had a good deal of salt in it when it appeared on the table, and yet somehow by putting *more* salt on before eating, the flavor seemed to be disguised enough to placate even my sensitive tongue.

The Sodium Mystique

It was while I worked as a laborer during a summer break in college that the importance of salt became established in my mind. Other college students and I were doing heavy work in the south Texas area where daily temperatures frequently hit 100° F in the shade, and, of course, no shade available. Our supervisor passed out white tablets to each of us, instructing us to take three a day. These were salt tablets. The theory was that through perspiration the body lost great amounts of salt during activity in the heat; salt tablets were supplied to make up that loss. Without salt, the body could not continue functioning.

That was all we were told at the time. There was a modicum of truth in it; there was a modicum of falsehood as well—as I was to learn later.

Without giving much thought to what purpose the salt tablets really served, we took the tablets day by day to keep ourselves from suffering heat collapse and heat prostration. I remember that the importance of salt in my summer work elevated the importance of salt in my mind, making me realize that my earlier aversion to it was obviously an erroneous prejudice due to improper upbringing.

In addition to that discovery, I had learned in chemistry classes that historically salt was a very late discovery of the human race, its introduction as a food flavoring occurring only six thousand years ago. Sanskrit, one of the oldest known human languages, did not even contain the word for salt. The word was introduced by the Greeks in one of its primitive dialects. It was then picked up from the Greeks by the Romans.

In the first three thousand years of its history, salt was a rare and almost esoteric product. It was known that the product could be obtained by drying up seawater. There were also hills of salt discovered in desert countries, particularly in the Mediterranean area. But it was still a rare and expensive commodity.

But it was definitely a commodity. Its first recorded use apparently was to conserve meat and fish from the rapid spoilage that occurred in desert heat. As its ability to preserve foodstuffs of various kinds became known to the ancient world, its use quickly increased. It became more valuable and consequently more expensive. Its use was not limited exclusively to preservation; people felt that its magical powers of preservation might be magical as well for humankind. Soon it became a "sacred" condiment.

In biblical times, it was used first in sacrifices to the gods. No one would dare to break a promise made over salt. "It is a covenant of salt for ever before the LORD unto thee and to thy seed with thee," the Bible states in Numbers 18:19. Salt was offered to Jehovah at harvest time in a sacrificial manner.

So rare was it in Roman times that army officers in foreign countries were paid an extra stipend to buy salt to flavor their food. Later on, the base of the Latin word *sal* was used in the word for pay itself, *salarium*, or salary.

People became used to the taste of salt in preserves and its usage spread everywhere. The Egyptians salted their coffins in the belief that it would help preserve their souls! Nomadic Arab tribes used salt to seal vows of undying loyalty. The Mesopotamians were so convinced of the power of salt that they considered it a holy substance.

As Good as Gold

In parts of Africa and in remote Tibet salt was once used as money, much like the Roman's use of the salt allowance. Herodotus describes a "salt" road stretching across the wastes of Libya: "At the distance of about ten days' journey from one another, heaps of salt in large lumps lie upon hills." Later: "At the distance of ten days' journey along the ridge of sand, there is a second salt hill." And so on. "Ten days' journey from Augila there is again a salt hill and a spring. . . . This region is inhabited by a nation called the Garmantians, a very powerful people, who cover the salt with mould, and then sow their crops." The salt hills extended all the way to the Pillars of Hercules, now called the Strait of Gibraltar.

In the Middle Ages, salt was just as rare and important as it had been in Roman times. Only kings and princes and lords and ladies were entitled to sprinkle salt on their food. The saltcellar was placed at a position of honor near the head of the table. The phrase "above the salt" came into use, referring to only the most important lords and ladies of the realm, those close enough to reach for the shaker.

And so the sodium mystique was born and grew. In the past three hundred years, salt became a food product that was well within reach of everyone. It became more than a preservative; it became a seasoning element that peasant and king alike could use. It was also discovered that the use of salt during cooking intensified the original taste of meats and vegetables. And it was discovered that salt used after cooking intensified subtle flavors too.

The importance of salt in politics became evident when hard-pressed monarchies in Europe began imposing salt taxes in order to gain revenue from people rich enough to use it. One of the first taxes abolished during the French Revolution was the extremely unpopular *gabelle*, the tax on salt. The British extracted levies from salt, particularly in India when the country was a colony. Its use was disallowed unless tariffs were paid.

It was Mahatma Gandhi, in fact, who used salt as a popular psychological blow against the British. In 1930 he started a three-week march to the sea. Once he was at the seashore, he picked up a lump of salt and licked it. Thousands who copied Gandhi's symbolic act were arrested and imprisoned for breaking the law.

The Constituents of Salt

Table salt is a chemical compound of two elements—*sodium*, a very reactive, soft, white, silvery metal; and *chlorine*, a toxic yellow-green gas. The chemical symbol for table salt is NaCl, the *Cl* standing for chloride, and the *Na* for the Latin word for sodium, *natrium*.

Thousands of years ago salt was usually obtained by the evaporation of seawater. It was also available underground and in surface deposits of rock salt. Many seas like the Dead Sea were coated with deposits of hard salt.

Aside from being used in cooking and at the table, which today makes up about only one-twentieth of its use, salt is employed to a large extent in the food-processing industry.

It is used to cure fish and meat; to form brine for pickles, olives, and sauerkraut; to enhance the leavening of bread in baking; and to improve the taste of many other ingredients.

Salt is also used to make cheese turn out the way the cheesemaker wants; salt controls fermentation. It also inhibits the growth of harmful bacteria in products like bacon, sausage, and bread.

Seasoned meat products like sausage are heavily laden with salt. The word *sausage* comes from Middle English *sausige*, from Old North French *saussiche*, from Lower Latin *salsicia*, originally from Latin *salsus*, meaning salted. The method of preserving meat in a packet, processed to keep it from spoiling, demands the use of salt in that process; the etymology of the word itself is fair warning. In no other kind of food is that message spelled out so clearly as in the word *sausage*.

Obviously, a product that has such a historical mystique must have some reason for being so important. Plainly it is not simply to flavor food for the palate, nor is it just for preservative purposes. Why is salt important to the body?

Sodium and Blood Pressure

Sodium actually forms part of the stomach's digestive juices, necessary to break down foods ingested into the body for use as energy. In particular, the absorption of sugars, amino acids, and water soluble vitamins (riboflavin, thiamin, and ascorbic acid) is dependent upon sodium. Sodium helps maintain what scientists call the osmotic pressure of the blood, which in turn maintains blood pressure. Sodium attracts water into the blood vessels, maintaining enough fluid for the proper blood volume and keeping the pressure of blood in the vessels constant. Sodium also helps to produce certain hormones in the body, especially those involved in the regulation of blood pressure.

Sodium helps maintain what is called the acid-base balance of the body. In combination with bicarbonate, potassium, and chloride, sodium adjusts the amount of acid and alkaline needed to keep the balance accurate. These chemicals work through the kidneys to perform this service.

Now, if salt is so important to the body, you may ask, why is there so much fuss being made about it now?

The answer is this: Like many other things in life, salt *must* be taken in moderation. *Only* in moderation can it be effective. If not enough salt is present, the human body can die. If too much salt is present, the same human body can also die.

Salt in excess and salt in dearth is a killer.

Salt in moderation—and as you will see later, this is a tiny amount—is a boon to mankind.

2

Hypertension: Target for a Killer

By the time I had been thoroughly fine-tuned by taste insensitivity to accommodate our salt-happy cuisine, certain voices in the wilderness had begun to broadcast facts about sodium that were disturbing to scientists in general and to nutritionists in particular.

Now that I was able to *enjoy* salted foods, the word came down that salt was a killer!

Actually, work regarding salt intake had been going on for some time in scientific circles, but so far nothing had leaked out to the public about the fact that overindulgence in salt was suspected of causing harm in certain people—in particular, in some of those afflicted with hypertension.

Hypertension is one of the world's most persistent killers. Simply put, hypertension is the medical word for high blood pressure, a disorder that can cause kidney failure, heart disease, and other ailments.

Over thirty-five million Americans, most studies show, suffer from hypertension. The reason the figure is only an

estimate is that millions have hypertension without actually knowing it. Of those who know they suffer from the
condition, many are not under treatment for it.

The Work of the Arterial System

In the most basic terms, the heart circulates blood through
the body's system of blood vessels to supply oxygen to the
tissues and remove impurities. To move that vital fluid
through the system requires a force sufficient to do the job.
That force is supplied by the pumping of the heart.

Blood pressure is the amount of push exerted against
the walls of the body's blood vessels during each heart beat.
Blood pressure is dependent in part upon the thickness of
the arteries that carry the blood. Their thickness is regulated by a complicated system of hormones and chemicals
that change the size of the vessels in accordance with the
needs of the body.

For example, when the body is resting, the arteries are
widened so that the blood is circulated more slowly and
easily through the body. When the body is active, the arteries narrow in order to force the blood through more
quickly.

However, in certain cases, the arteries become perma-
nently narrow. The heart then has to move the same
amount of blood to all parts of the body through a system
of thinner carriers, causing the heart to labor much harder
to do the job.

Continual high blood pressure puts a greater strain on
the heart and in turn eventually can cause heart failure,
fatal heart attacks, strokes that paralyze, and ruin to the
kidneys as well.

In some cases, the entire human system becomes frozen in a high blood pressure mode. The system loses its ability to expand or contract the arteries and remains in a permanent contracted situation. This unfortunate condition is called high blood pressure, or hypertension. That is, the tension of the blood vessels is "hyper," or higher than normal.

Hypertension endangers the health and elasticity of the arteries, overworks the heart, causes the brain to lack the proper nourishment of fresh blood, and threatens the efficiency of the kidneys in eliminating waste from the system.

The higher the blood pressure, the shorter the life expectancy.

Getting a Fix on Blood Pressure

Blood pressure is measured by a device called a sphygmomanometer. This is a cuff or a covered, inflatable rubber bladder attached to a measuring device. The examiner wraps an appropriate-sized cuff around the upper arm and inflates the device to stop blood flow in the main arteries. The air is then let out of the cuff.

At this point, the blood once again flows through the arteries after having been cut off by the cuff. The measurement records the two principal actions involving the heart. It squeezes to push blood; it relaxes to rest.

The force of its flow at the time it squeezes is called the *systolic* pressure. The force of its flow at the time it rests is called the *diastolic* pressure. The sphygmomanometer measures both systolic and diastolic pressure. The measurement is calibrated on the meter.

There are two numbers in any blood-pressure measure: systolic and diastolic. The average reading for the normal healthy adult is about 120/80 (systolic/diastolic), but it can vary in different people. It all depends on age, condition of the arteries, and medical history. By the time the reading gets up to 160/95, it is considered too high for comfort. The condition is considered hypertension, or high blood pressure.

Very little is actually known about the cause of hypertension. Many cases cannot be analyzed properly. But it is a known fact that hypertension that is not controlled can cause serious problems.

Targets for Hypertension

Certain people tend to be affected by hypertension more than others—people with specific physical builds, people who work at special jobs, people with stressful lifestyles, people who eat incontinently, and so on.

Generally speaking, here are the groups that seem targeted for hypertension much more preponderantly than other types:

- Men are subject to hypertension more than women until age sixty-five when this reverses. When men have hypertension, it is usually in a more severe form.
- Women who are pregnant may tend to develop hypertension more than those who are not. Women also tend to develop high blood pressure while taking birth-control pills.
- Blacks are twice as apt to be afflicted by hypertension as whites. When they get it, often at a younger age than whites, they are more severely affected by it, especially male blacks.

- Short, heavy people, or those who are overweight, are more prone to hypertension than people who are slender and lightweight.
- Hypertension seems to be hereditary. Relatives of people already afflicted with hypertension, it is thought, are more liable to be affected by high blood pressure.
- People whose blood pressure tends to vary between normal and high values are called prehypertensives or "labile hypertensives." Three out of four of these people will usually develop hypertension.
- People who lead lives of continual frustration and stress tend to be hypertensive, but only if they are prone to it. Removing stress may help those with such tendencies.

Two Types of Hypertension

There are two basic kinds of hypertension. One is called primary, essential, or idiopathic hypertension, and the other, secondary hypertension.

Essential hypertension is diagnosed when the causative factors of the disease are as yet unknown, and this is the explanation in 90 to 95 percent of cases. The course of the disease may be a relatively slow one.

Secondary hypertension is diagnosed when the cause has been demonstrated—usually due to a kidney or endocrine abnormality. A cause for hypertension usually occurs in only 5 to 10 percent of cases. The internal organs have deteriorated to a degree, but blood pressure may return to normal once the causative factors have been corrected.

Both types of the disease are dangerous. Either may cause severe tissue damage very quickly and without much warning; this is malignant hypertension. The internal damage from hypertension can manifest itself in at least six different ways:

- *Arteriosclerosis*. This is a hardening and scarring of the outer walls of the arteries that can follow untreated hypertension.
- *Atherosclerosis*. This is a buildup of fat and other materials inside the walls of the arteries. It will impede the flow of blood through the already constricted vessels.
- *Heart attack.* The heart, pumping harder and becoming enlarged, is less effective. Because of clogged arteries, it may not receive enough blood to pump. The result may be a heart attack.
- *Stroke.* The brain, starved of blood because of narrowed arteries, may be afflicted by a stroke. Permanent brain damage may result.
- *Blindness.* The eyes can be affected by hypertension. If the blood vessels in the eyes are constantly strained and swollen by high blood pressure, blindness may eventually result.
- *Kidney damage.* The kidneys cannot remove body wastes through arteries that have hardened. The wastes build up in the blood, eventually poisoning the entire body.

Certain symptoms of hypertension occur as warning signals, but many people do not realize exactly what they mean. In fact, each of the symptoms, taken separately, does *not* mean hypertension is necessarily present. Some of these telltale signs are as follows:

- *Dizziness.* If the diastolic pressure is about 110, dizziness may indicate the presence of hypertension.

- *Nosebleeds.* If the nose bleeds without apparent cause, it may point to hypertension.
- *Headaches.* If they are severe, if they are of recent origin, if they are localized in one specific part of the head, if they occur in early morning, if they are accompanied by nausea, and if vision becomes progressively worse, headaches can point to hypertension.
- *Breathlessness.*

NOTE: Fainting is definitely *not* a sign of hypertension. It is much more likely to indicate exactly the opposite—the presence of low blood pressure, or hypotension.

Early Studies of Hypertension

At the turn of the century, the internal workings of hypertension and its causes were being studied by various scientists and physicians. The studies were largely unproductive. It was thought that high blood pressure resulted from overweight and lack of exercise. Later it was thought to be a result of eating too many fried foods. The real villain or villains had not been isolated.

In 1904 two French scientists, Ambard and Beaujard, published a paper in one of the best French medical journals of the time, discussing hypertension. It was their theory—and a revolutionary one it was—that common table salt was the villain in the disorder. Their paper included a special new low-salt diet which they said had been used effectively to reduce high blood pressure in patients.

Unfortunately, while the paper was to the point, it was

short and somewhat scientifically skimpy, with little scientific evidence to back up their findings. Most scientists simply passed it up as another crackpot idea. For that reason, the theory that salt was a killer did not emerge from the scientific world into the real world, and as a consequence the public was completely unaware of it.

Then in 1920 F. M. Allen, a specialist in kidney disorders, published a textbook on the treatment of renal diseases. In his book he presented scientific data that showed how successful a low-sodium regimen could be in the treatment of high blood pressure. Since the material was contained in a scientific textbook that was not generally available to the public and received no publicity at all, the public once again did not find out about low-sodium diets.

The "Rice House" That Kempner Built

In 1940 Walter Kempner, a researcher at Duke University, began treating 140 patients with high blood pressure, using a special diet he had created. Kempner's aim was to try to halt the progressive destruction of the heart, the kidneys, and the eyes in hypertensive patients.

The diet consisted of rice, fruit juice, vitamins, and iron. It became known popularly as the rice diet, for the sake of simplicity. His offices where he treated his patients were known as the rice house.

Kempner presented findings four years later on May 3, 1944. The results were astounding. Generally, his patients found that their elevated pressures were markedly reduced. Some enlarged hearts were returned to their normal function. The deterioration in the eyes that usually led to complete blindness had been arrested in many cases. Damaged retinas healed.

Although such a discovery should have caused the world to take the rice diet to its heart, it did not. Actually, an almost insurmountable problem accompanied Kempner's rice diet. The diet was simply so monotonous and dull that most patients could not tolerate it. The rice and fruit did not really taste very good. Also, a patient had to keep on the diet for a relatively long period of time before any results became apparent.

Hospitalization was needed until blood pressure could be controlled. Urine and blood tests were taken repeatedly. Modifications of the diet were tried, but none worked. The result of Kempner's diet was that it was so awful-tasting that the only excuse for its existence was the fact that it worked.

No one really knew why. Scientists focused on rice to analyze its content. Was it the essential ingredient of the diet? Perhaps rice had low cholesterol values. Was it weight loss alone? The dieters certainly lost weight. But no one could guess why the diet actually cured high blood pressure in most of the cases.

It was not until some time later that lab technicians and nutritionists finally solved the problem. It wasn't the rice; it wasn't the fruit. Nor was it the vitamins or the pills.

It was the absence of salt.

The rice diet that Kempner had put together allowed very little sodium to be ingested, not through any specific purpose but simply by accident. It was not the rice but the absence of salt that made the diet so amazingly effective.

That raised the ghost of Ambard and Beaujard's earlier low-salt diet. Kempner's diet was compared with that of Ambard and Beaujard for effectiveness. Soon it was determined that both of the diets worked. Effects of a high-salt diet were also studied. In some cases the intake of salt actually elevated blood pressure.

Was salt—or at least sodium, one of its constituents—indeed a killer?

3

Studies in Salt Consumption

At about the time I was congratulating myself on acquiring a taste for salt and beginning to enjoy heavily spiced and seasoned foods, other scientists were just beginning to find out the truth about this villain that masqueraded as a hero.

Although the Kempner rice diet did isolate one particularly relevant variable in the fight against hypertension—the absence of salt in the diet—it did not conclusively prove that salt was the central villain in the hypertension story. It was obvious to other scientists that there were really a number of elements in the diet that made it effective for sufferers of high blood pressure.

There were three main points to consider.

- First, the diet forced the patient to lose weight. The lack of fat and adequate proteins in the diet contributed to a temporary loss of corpulence in the body. Certainly

loss of weight helped cut down hypertension. The medical fraternity had known that for some time.
- Second, the diet was high in potassium. The presence of fruits and vegetables provided a great deal of potassium to the sufferers of hypertension. The actual role of potassium in the cure of hypertension was not known clearly.
- And, third, as I have mentioned, the diet was low in salt. And the role of salt in hypertension was not known to any degree of accuracy.

Nevertheless, the importance of the lack of salt content in the diet was a breakthrough for specialists. It got them thinking in a new direction at last. The diet had a little something for advocates of almost every dietary stricture known. Frederic Barter of the Veterans Administration Hospital in San Antonio commented that "Kempner's diet is so confounded that you can't say its effects are solely due to its low sodium content." But it did put nutritionists on the track of salt intake and its effects on the human body.

Tracking Down the Killer

The main problem specialists faced in evaluating these results, then, was the fact that no other animals except humans suffered from high blood pressure. Most tests were made on animals rather than man, for obvious reasons. Researchers could not test a low-salt diet on animals to analyze its effectiveness against hypertension since the disease was unknown to them.

However, one investigator at Vanderbilt University, George

R. Meneely, began to feed experimental rats salt-flavored food in their daily diets. Within seventeen months, not all, but a majority, of his lab rats had developed high blood pressure from the ingestion of large amounts of salt. Many of the rats even died from it.

The normal life span of a lab rat is between twenty-four and forty-eight months, an average of thirty-six months. Salt had cut the life span of some of the rats almost in half at seventeen months.

Autopsies of these experimental animals showed excessive kidney damage and enlargement of the heart, exactly the kind of deterioration experienced in human beings with hypertension. The hypertensive rats died of pneumonia, heart attack, and strokes—an amazingly similar parallel to the possible causes of death in human beings afflicted with hypertension.

Meneely's team had created hypertension in the animal world by forcing animals to eat something they would not have obtained in their diets in the first place. It meant that hypertension might not be caused simply by stress and emotional strain but might be caused by the intake of certain foodstuffs.

On the average, the team found that some of the animals had begun to experience hypertension after only nine months of a salty diet. Nine months in a rat's life was equivalent to the beginning of middle age in a human being's. Statistics showed that the period of first signs of hypertension corresponded almost exactly to the time when hypertension manifested itself in the human species.

Meneely's team had fed their test animals with an amount of salt almost equivalent to the amount of salt used by the average person in America—from 6 to 10 grams per day (1¼ to 2 teaspoons).

Creating the Hypertensive-Prone Animal

About this time another scientist, Lewis K. Dahl, became interested in experiments similar to Meneely's. He found it hard to believe that rats living on a salt-intake diet equivalent to that of a human being would develop hypertension at such a high rate of speed. However, at the same time, he realized that not all the rats involved in the experiment had become hypertensive at all. Obviously, there were some individual differences.

Dahl paralleled Meneely's experiments, finding that many of the rats did become hypertensive during their first nine months of life. These he isolated as hypertensive-prone types and let them mature. He then mated hypertensive-prones with one another. A majority of the offspring of these matings were found to be hypertensive-prone too. By the time Dahl had gone through three generations, he had produced a generation in which *all* members were hypertensive-prone. He had, in effect, genetically created a hypertensive-prone animal!

The lesson was obvious. High blood pressure was genetically transmittable, at least in animals. Assuming that the same biological and physiological factors were at work in the human race, it could be asserted that high blood pressure in human beings was genetically transmittable too.

That meant that any person with hypertensive relatives would also, in all probability, be prone to hypertension too!

The main question Dahl was trying to answer had not yet been answered. What he wanted to know was whether or not a low-salt or no-salt diet could prevent or allay the appearance of hypertension in a laboratory animal that was hypertensive-prone.

His next step was to test the results of a high-salt diet on two sets of animals: one prone by heredity to hypertension and another *not* prone to hypertension by heredity. Sure enough, the animals prone to hypertension developed it. Those that were resistant did not.

Dahl then went to the next and final step in the experiment. He had now bred two separate strains of laboratory animals, one susceptible to hypertension and another resistant to hypertension.

He used fourth-generation animals and fed both sets of them a diet that did not have any salt in it at all. The animals that had been bred to develop hypertension did *not* do so. Nor did the animals resistant to hypertension.

The test was now complete. It provided evidence that a low-salt diet could prevent the onset of hypertension in a group of experimental animals that had been bred to develop high blood pressure. The points proved by the experiment could now be applied to human beings to see if similar results could be obtained.

Hypertensives and Non-Hypertensives

Dahl himself decided to study human beings in a community in New York after concluding his animal studies. He began some simple human experiments by categorizing 897 adults into three different classes:

- One category included those with low salt intake. These were people who never added salt to their food.
- A second category included those with an average in-

take of salt. They added salt to food only after tasting it to see if it was sufficiently salty.

• A third category included those with a high salt intake. These customarily added salt to food before tasting anything.

Of the 897 people studied, 71 of them were hypertensives, about 8 percent. Of the 71 hypertensives, only one was in the low intake of salt category. Forty of the hypertensives belonged in the third category, that of high intake of salt. The rest, thirty, were in the middle group.

This was supportive evidence of his theory, but was it universal?

Other Studies of Salt Intake in Humans

In further studies of human subjects Dahl found evidence to prove his theory by examining the salt intake of people in various countries.

In Japan, for example, Dahl discovered that in the Akita Province in the north of Japan, the average daily consumption of sodium chloride was almost three and a half to six teaspoons a day, much higher than the intake in America. These Japanese farmers had for years preserved their food with salt, and were used to consuming large quantities of it. For comparison's sake, six teaspoons of salt is equivalent to about 30 grams, or 30,000 milligrams, of sodium chloride.

Interestingly enough, statistics showed that almost 40 percent of the farmers in Akita were afflicted with high blood pressure. Many of them died of it, usually in the form of strokes. At the age of fifty, almost 67 percent—two out of every three people—were afflicted with hypertension.

These findings bore out Dahl's discoveries about the correlation of high salt intake and hypertension in rats.

In order to balance out the study, Dahl found that Japanese farmers living in the southern part of Japan ate only about one-half to two-thirds of the amount of salt their northern compatriots did. Some of the southern Japanese were afflicted by hypertension, but only about two in ten, about 20 percent.

Dahl correlated observations of other scientists as well.

In the Solomon Islands in the South Pacific, two tribes were observed, each similar to the other in most respects except for the high incidence of hypertension in one of them and the low incidence in the other.

The two tribes lived in different parts of the Solomon Islands Archipelago. One tribe, the Lau, lived on a lagoon. The other, the Ontong Javans, lived in villages in the hills. Among the lagoon people there was a high incidence of high blood pressure. The average incidence rose with advancing age. Many died of the effects of hypertension.

The hill people did not have any significant incidence of high blood pressure at all. Nor did the hill people succumb to hypertension with advancing age, as the lagoon people did.

Both tribes ate pretty much the same kind of food. They had the same exercise, and their lifestyles were similar. There was only one significant difference: The lagoon people, the Lau tribe, boiled their vegetables in sea water. Because of their method of cooking, they would habitually ingest about 15 to 20 grams of salt a day (3 to 4 teaspoons). The hill people, the Ontong Javans, boiled their vegetables in rainwater or well water. Because of their method of cooking in fresh water, they would habitually ingest almost no salt at all.

Lot Page, chief of medicine at Newton-Wellesley Hospital,

who had made the studies of the Solomon Islanders, believed that the evidence at hand about salt intake was convincing enough to recommend that people watch their intake from infancy onward.

"The strongest correlation is with sodium consumption," Page said. "Weight comes out as important too, but not nearly so much as lack of sodium in the diet."

Other studies have been made on more than twenty cultures, including the Eskimos, the Kikuyu tribe in Kenya, and fighters of the Masai tribe in East Africa.

The Eskimos were discovered to be the most carnivorous eaters among the human race. The average Eskimo consumed about 6,000 calories each day—three times the intake of the average American. About 4,500 calories, or about 4½ pounds, came from the meat, and 1,500 calories from fat. Yet in spite of the prodigious intake of protein and fat, the Eskimos had a low incidence of hypertension. Heart attacks were rare. Also there was evidence that Eskimos metabolize fat differently than other racial groups.

The Yanomamo Indians of Brazil, isolated from civilization by hundreds of miles, ate relatively no salt and had little sodium intake daily; they were remarkably free of cases of hypertension.

The King Bushmen of the Kalahari Desert, another isolated tribe miles away from civilization and salt, were also free of cases of hypertension.

Among the Bantu tribe in South Africa, the average tribesman consumed about eighteen grams of sodium daily, and there was a hypertension incidence of about 25 percent.

In the Marshall Islands, the tribesmen consumed about seven grams of sodium daily, with a 7 percent incidence of hypertension.

Taken altogether, the studies Dahl investigated showed

that hypertension was virtually absent in any population that used small amounts of salt. Conversely, in cultures where a lot of salt was consumed, a higher percentage of people was found to develop the disease.

Analyzing the findings more specifically, scientists discovered that an intake of about 1.7 grams of sodium a day (slightly less than 1/16 of an ounce), aside from the sodium that occurred naturally in all foods, was enough to trigger hypertension.

However, Dahl knew that the population studies were a bit inconclusive inasmuch as the lifestyle of the tribes studied varied so much from the lifestyle of the average American. An industrialized people tended to be less physically active than nonindustrialized people. Also Americans were more prone to the stress of modern life. Primitive groups were not. These factors, as well as low-salt intake, would help to account for the absence of high blood pressure in the more remote societies.

Was it tied exclusively to salt?

Potassium and Weight

Not everyone agreed conclusively that hypertension was linked irrevocably to salt intake. Harriet Dustan of the University of Alabama Medical School, a past president of the American Heart Association, noted three differences, other than salt consumption, between primitive and industrialized societies that might mean the difference in the incidence of hypertension.

"In societies like the United States, people gain weight with age," she pointed out. "In primitive societies, they lose weight with age. Blood pressure and weight are highly cor-related—there didn't need to be another study about that."

The second difference she noted was in potassium in-take. "In primitive societies people eat relatively more po-tassium than in industrialized societies," she said. Third, people in primitive societies tended to be physically fit—much more so than the average American.

"We don't know the importance of that observation," she admitted. However, one study by Danish researchers showed a relationship between physical conditioning and hyper-tension after correcting for other variables such as body weight.

"We are talking about a very complex issue," she said in discussing speculation about why primitive peoples have less hypertension than Americans.

Salt as Villain

Other scientists became interested in the observations of Dahl and thus began to confirm and refine his early impres-sions.

Kawasaki and his colleagues in 1978 gave either low- or high-salt diets to patients with hypertension. They were able to identify those among the group who behaved as either salt-sensitive or salt-resistant, as had been done with Dahl's rats.

In other experiments recently, salt reduction as a method of treatment for mild hypertension was used by at least three groups of scientists. Parijis, Morgan, and MacGregor, along with their colleagues, demonstrated that blood pres-sure could be reduced even if salt was restricted for one month. The blood pressure reduction wasn't large, but the reduced risk of danger to the patients was on the order of 10 to 15 percent. Unlike Kawasaki's work, the patients were not classified as salt-sensitive or salt-resistant hypertensives.

In 1982 Trevor C. Beard and his co-workers in Australia studied the effect of a low-salt diet in patients receiving medication for mild hypertension. During the twelve-week study the blood pressure decreased in the group treated with medicine and a low-salt diet as well as in the group treated with medicine and unrestricted salt diet. But at the end of the study the group with the low-salt diet had one in three patients off medication and the medicine dose stopped or reduced in four out of five patients.

It was becoming clear that salt was a contributor to hypertension—at a minimum, one of perhaps several causative factors yet to be clearly identified. Further, it appeared that salt was a villain that could be controlled.

Now it was time to do something, to set up standards that would enable people to isolate the killer and protect daily intake against this insidious murderer that posed as a friend of man.

4

The Killer
Isolated:
Sodium

By the time the experiments devised by Meneely, Kempner and Dahl had been assimilated by scientists and nutritionists, it was obvious that further studies would have to be made to analyze the effects of salt, potassium, and diet in general. A series of facts began to emerge which shaped nutritional aims for the next several years.

From my experience I learned that many people know little about salt except that they have acquired a taste for it through the pressures of living in our civilized society. In fact, most people have never really heard the word *sodium* except in chemistry class.

To clear up one misconception right away, the symbol *Na* stands for sodium, rather than a more logical *So* might. In fact, the word *sodium* was a manufactured one, based on the English *soda*, entering the vocabulary through New Latin, the Latin used after the Middle Ages especially in scientific work. The people devising the chemical symbols had opted for the sign *Na*, from the Latin *natrium*, a word used for soda in Roman times. Also, it is important to remember that table salt is NaCl, as almost everyone with a high school education knows. In other words, table salt is a combination of sodium and chloride.

Salt = Sodium + Chloride

Through the reports of studies of ancient peoples and their rates of salt intake, a great deal of confusion was inadvertently spread by the interchange of the word *salt* with the word *sodium*. Sodium is *not* equal to salt either in quantity or quality. Salt is composed of approximately 40 percent sodium and 60 percent chloride. So that confusion is not perpetuated, I use salt and sodium chloride interchangeably. In the experiments made by the nutritionists, it was the *sodium* that turned out to be important, not the salt itself or the chloride. Whenever I discuss sodium, it is the element and its amount expressed as a weight.

Even more importantly, a lot of sodium was found to occur in food, much of which does not taste salty at all and, in fact, that has the *opposite* taste. For example, it is pretty obvious that bacon has salt in it. It *tastes* salty. But chocolate pudding doesn't taste salty; it tastes sweet. Yet, from a scientific standpoint, sweet pudding actually has a great deal more sodium than bacon. A lot of strange findings came out:

- One-half cup of chocolate-flavored instant pudding contains 470 milligrams of sodium. Two slices of bacon contain only 245. Thus, one serving of sweet pudding contains 225 more milligrams of sodium than a two-slice serving of bacon.

- By making a sandwich with two slices of beef and pork bologna sausage in between two slices of white bread, an extra 440 milligrams of sodium would be added to the 284 milligrams in the bread—for a grand total of 724 milligrams.

In addition to these discoveries and others similar to them, I found out another important and quite revealing truth. As I said before, sodium is used in preservation and in processing. But it is also used in certain kinds of diet drinks. For example, while an 8-ounce bottle of *low-calorie* carbonated fruit drink contains 46 milligrams of sodium, an 8-ounce bottle of carbonated fruit drink contains only 34 milligrams. It was obvious that in some instances the substitution of a low-calorie substance is simply an exchange of sodium for carbohydrate. But if weight loss is more important to achieve than severe sodium restriction, small difference in amount of sodium may not be important.

On the other hand, many low-calorie foods contain little sodium. To find out how much became a matter of continually checking the labels carefully.

Too Much Salt for Comfort

Processing foods for instant cooking involves the introduction of large amounts of sodium, usually in the form of disodium phosphate. I found that instant breakfast cereal usually contains many more milligrams of sodium than the regular old-fashioned cereal that took more time to cook. Again, it is necessary to look on the label to find out exactly how much sodium was used in its preparation.

It was not difficult for nutritionists to find out exactly how much sodium the human body needed to survive. It was finally decided that it took no more than 220 milligrams (.008 ounces) of sodium a day in order to sustain life. However, on the average, most Americans consumed almost *twenty times* that amount.

In fact, some estimates held that the average daily dietary intake of some Americans was as high as 8,000 to 12,000 milligrams of sodium, more than fifty times as much as was needed by the body. The average fell around 4,000 or 5,000. These figures were greatly in excess of the *bare essential minimum* figure of 220 milligrams.

"Need" could be ascertained at about 1,200 milligrams of sodium a day, much over the bare minimum, but far, far less than average.

In a series of tests, the National Research Council of the National Academy of Sciences determined in 1979 that an "adequate and safe" sodium intake equaled 1,100 to 3,300 milligrams a day for adults, that is, about 1.1 to 3.3 grams of sodium, or about 2.82 to 8.46 grams of table salt. (The conversion for this is 1 teaspoon of salt = 5 g. of NaCl = 2,132 mg. of sodium.) In other words, the "adequate and safe intake" amounted to about one-fourth the 4 to 5 grams of sodium even the average American consumed. Thus a wide range between absolute minimum and a tolerable average was found.

It was also found that an excess of sodium consumption did not create problems in human beings *in all cases*, but did so in certain people who corresponded to the hypertensive-prones in Dahl's experiments with animals. The question was to determine at what point the intake of sodium became harmful enough to them to trigger hypertension.

After a great deal of study and testing, a guideline for nutritionists was finally drawn up and a series of figures prepared for the public. Although no specific figure was ever determined, it was estimated that by the time a potentially hypertensive individual had consumed some 1,700 to 2,000 milligrams of sodium per day on a regular basis, the body might react by developing high blood pressure. The figure spread was definitely an estimate, but seemed a practical one.

The point was that most people did not realize what 2,000 milligrams of sodium *looked like* in actual foodstuffs. For example, a single serving of canned chicken noodle soup—say one cup—supplies at least half a day's allowance of sodium. Other processed foods—some cheese, tomato juice, canned tuna, salad dressing, breakfast cereals, ice cream, and bread—also contain significant quantities of sodium that remain hidden from view.

Sodium and the Human Body— a Profile

One of the things that intrigued me was the actual status of sodium itself. Was it a poison to the body of a hypertensive as the studies seemed to indicate? How much could be eliminated to provide for a total control of hypertension?

I knew it couldn't be completely eliminated to provide for a total control of hypertension. The body *does* need a certain amount of sodium. It is essential to life itself, as briefly discussed earlier. My next question led me into a re-examination of the actual workings of the human body and how it utilizes the sodium it needs to function.

First of all, sodium is a most important nutrient, along

with potassium and chloride. Without any one of these three, the human body would not survive.

The job of sodium is to regulate the amount of water and electrolytes in and out of body cells. The body has devised a most complex system to maintain the proper flow of blood to and from the heart. The system works by means of hormones, chemicals, and signals by the nervous system. These components of the system in turn regulate the width of the blood vessels that carry oxygen and food from the arteries to the tissues of the body. Blood vessels are called arterioles, and the system itself is known as the arteriole system.

If part of the body needs a lot of food at a particular moment—let's suppose in the digestive tract during the night—the system signals the arterioles in the area of the stomach and intestines to expand and encourage an increase in the flow of blood to activate the digestive system in these organs. At the same time, the system signals the rest of the body to restrict or contract the arterioles elsewhere. That balance is essential in order not to *overwork* the entire body when only the stomach needs attention.

It is obvious that such a complex system is apt to go awry if all factors are not exactly and strictly regulated. What does happen in certain individuals is exactly that. The regulatory system sometimes goes bad. Arterioles, or blood vessels, *all over the body* constrict at the same time and stay constricted, when only one area might need sustenance.

What happens when the arterioles are constricted is that the pressure in the larger arteries goes up and stays up as the heart tries to force the blood through the thinned channels and smaller diameters of the arteries. That causes an abnormal elevation of blood pressure all over the body.

The Sodium-Potassium Balance

Scientists found during their experiments that while sodium tends to help the arteriole system constrict the arteries, potassium helps the system enlarge them. To be more accurate, salt intake elevates blood pressure less if potassium is present than if it is not. Potassium is in no way a preventive of hypertension, but its presence does counteract the effects of salt in raising the blood pressure.

In fact, increased potassium intake *improves* the effectiveness of low-salt diets in lowering the blood pressure. Potassium, it was found, even exerts a sedative effect on the nervous systems of hypertensive subjects.

However, it was not a total solution to the problem. Nor did anyone really understand how the sodium/potassium balance works. There were theories. The most commonly accepted view was that sodium affects the body through its ability to retain water. The retention of water in the body is of absolute necessity in order to give the blood fluid enough to keep it in flowing condition. Without enough, the blood slacks off and not enough of it gets to the parts of the body needing nutriment and oxygen.

In fact, it was established that sodium and potassium seem to create a special balance between retention of fluid and the elimination of fluid. Theorists attributed the need for the sodium/potassium balance to the early evolution of the human body millions of years ago. In the diets of early man, which contained large amounts of meats and fruits and vegetables, a great deal of potassium was present. It was *sodium* that was in low quantity.

The environment, to put it another way, was a low-sodium, high-potassium one. Thus the body's regulatory mechanism was originally engineered to hang onto its sodium because of its scarcity, and to excrete its potassium because of its more consistent availability in the individual's food intake.

Through the years the bodily mechanism, especially in the function of the kidneys, did not change. It excreted potassium freely in the urine, but held onto its sodium, letting it out only through perspiration and chiefly the urine, but in vastly smaller quantities than potassium.

Through the millions of years of mankind's evolution, diet changed considerably. The small need for sodium, dictated by the bodily mechanism and its minimal presence in animal meat, fruits, and vegetables, became filled immediately with table salt for seasoning and processed foods.

With the advance in food processing in the last hundred years, people's sodium intake increased dramatically. While human beings added more salt in the interest of flavor and preservation, they inadvertently reduced the natural concentrations of potassium by excessively processing meats, grains, fruits and vegetables. Thus the intake of potassium shrank somewhat because of changing lifestyles. Primitive people, with their primitive bodies, tended to retain the proper balance of sodium to potassium. Civilized people, with their primitive bodies little changed, tend to upset the balance by their style of eating.

Sodium's Role in
the Hypertensive-Prone

Now, getting back to the human body in today's world, the excess sodium taken in affects certain individuals by creating an imbalance in fluid, that is by holding onto more fluid than is absolutely necessary. However, in the majority of individuals, the body's regulatory mechanism is able to neutralize this imbalance. Those people are able to control excess sodium through natural bodily checks.

It is the *other* people—as a minimum, the 10 or 12 percent of the population born with a predilection to hypertension—that cannot control excess sodium. These are the hypertensive-prones that Dahl discovered in his experiments.

In a hypertensive-prone, consuming the average large amount of sodium—or, let's say, a large amount of sodium in the 8,000 to 12,000 milligram-a-day area—the bodily mechanism becomes saturated with sodium. With the sodium doing its duty in the sodium to potassium to chloride balance by retaining an excess of bodily fluid, bodily weight would *increase* by the excess fluid.

At the same time, with an excess of fluid in the blood, the volume of blood is greater than needed. The arterial system thus is *overburdened* with excess blood volume. The result is a situation conducive to high blood pressure.

A One-Two Punch to the Heart

In addition to expanding the volume of blood pumped by the heart, sodium was also found to act in one other specific way. It has the ability to constrict the small blood vessels, our old friends the arterioles. By providing an excess of fluid in the blood, and by constricting the arterioles, sodium thus provides a one-two punch to the heart. The heart is forced to work harder to push the expanded volume of blood through the narrowed channels in the arteriole system.

This added burden on the heart causes the individual

the most harm. Such an added pressure on the heart winds up causing some kind of breakdown of the system: heart attack, stroke, or kidney complication resulting from hypertension.

Although these factors caused by sodium—excess fluid and constriction of the arteries—do not cause trouble in the average nonhypertensive-prone individual (the body simply excretes the superfluous amounts of sodium and the condition disappears), they can cause hypertension in the hypertensive-prone adult.

Hypertension induced by this excess of sodium and allowed to persist unchecked through the years can seriously damage arteries and kidneys, even causing the heart to enlarge and fail completely.

Although high blood pressure may not be the result in all hypertensive-prones, it may cause a problem of some sort. Because there are large gaps in man's knowledge about the body, I found that the full story of sodium could not be evaluated even after all the studies were finished.

However, I did learn that it was established to the satisfaction of many other physicians and nutritionists that in the case of certain hypertensives, their tendency to develop high blood pressure can be brought down by eating a diet containing virtually no salt.

Unknowns in the Sodium Mystery

There are many factors about sodium that are still unknown even today. The Federation of American Societies for Experimental Biology Select Committee (FASEB) on substances "generally recognized as safe" (GRAS) estimated that from 10 to 30 percent of all Americans are born with a genetic predisposition to hypertension. When that genetic factor is present, a diet high in sodium increases the risk of hypertension. Scientists feel that if sodium consumption is high, the effects of other factors that are associated with high blood pressure may be intensified.

Even the Surgeon General's *Report on Health Promotion and Disease Prevention* in 1979 maintained that all Americans would "probably be healthier as a whole" if they made several dietary changes, including a reduction in salt.

"Few experts claim that salt is the sole cause of hypertension," said the Harvard Medical School *Health Letter* in 1979. "Rather, they describe salt as an important contributing factor in the 10 to 20 percent of Americans who are genetically susceptible to high blood pressure. And for such persons, the hidden salt in processed food of the typical American diet is a real hazard."

Whether the number of Americans with a predisposition to hypertension is 10 to 30 percent as FASEB maintained, or 10 to 20 percent as the Harvard *Letter* maintained, matters little. I became a believer some time before.

The next step was to come to grips with the sodium in my patients and my own diet and rout it out!

5

Tracking Down the Villain

Like catching the murderer in a whodunit, the real problem in effectively cutting down on sodium intake is not exclusively in putting the saltcellar back in the kitchen cabinet, but in finding out by a process of deduction and investigation exactly where the villain is hiding out.

The assumption that the problem is sodium is certainly a giant step forward in the game. But it is only the first step in isolating and tracking it down.

I was astounded at the many different guises in which sodium appears in our foods. (Remember, sodium is not synonymous with salt.) A partial list of additives in food that contain sodium makes a formidable compendium of harmful sources.

Danger: Hidden Sodium

The most common food additives containing sodium are these:

- *Baking powder.* This mixture contains amounts of sodium and is used in the preparation of breads and cakes as a leavening agent. Along with sodium, it contains starch, flour, and carbonates.
- *Baking soda.* This is sodium bicarbonate, or bicarbonate of soda, and is used, like baking powder, in the preparation of breads, cakes, and sometimes in the cooking of vegetables. It is also used as an alkalizer in cases of indigestion. It must be counted in all such uses because of its very large concentration of sodium.
- *Brine.* Table salt and water combined form brine, used in processing foods and in canning, freezing, and pickling.
- *Disodium phosphate.* Watch out for instant cereals and quick-cooking foods of all kinds. If disodium phosphate is used, the instant food resulting contains sodium. Disodium phosphate is also used in the processing of cheese.
- *Monosodium glutamate* (MSG). This is a seasoning used in restaurant cooking and sometimes in home cooking. It also occurs in many packaged, canned, and processed frozen foods as a taste intensifier. Next to table salt, it is the most common type of sodium because it occurs in restaurant cooking with great frequency, particularly in Chinese foods.
- *Salt.* This is sodium chloride, the common table salt used in seasoning, cooking, canning, and other types of food processing. It is the most common form of sodium and the one with the highest profile. Beware! One teaspoon of salt contains nearly 2 grams of sodium.

- *Sodium alginate.* This is a chemical used in chocolate milk and ice cream to provide a smooth texture that pleases the tongue and palate.
- *Sodium benzoate.* This is used as a preservative in condiments like relishes, salad dressings, and sauces of all kinds.
- *Sodium hydroxide.* This is used in the processing of foods like fruits and vegetables, in hominy, and in ripe olives. It loosens the skin and softens the produce for eating.
- *Sodium nitrate (and nitrite).* This is an additive also known as saltpeter, used not only to preserve but to cure meat as well. It is frequently found in steaks of all kinds, beef and ham included. Also bacon. It is extremely difficult to find cured or processed meats free of this substance in most conventional supermarkets.
- *Sodium propionate.* This is used in pasteurized cheeses and in some breads and cakes to cut down on the growth of mold.
- *Sodium sulfite.* This is used as a bleach for some fresh fruits like glazed or crystallized produce, and as a preservative for some dried fruits like prunes.

NOTE: Water and medicines must be considered as suppliers of unwanted sodium. Tap water usually contains sodium, sometimes in quantities as large as 100 milligrams a cup, but mostly about 5 to 10 milligrams a cup. It may be necessary to investigate to find out how much sodium your own city water contains. The use of a water softener definitely adds sodium to the water from the tap. It is best to find out exactly how much sodium the water softener adds. Even simple products like patent medicines—aspirin and Alka-Seltzer—contain quantities of sodium that can throw off a carefully constructed low-sodium diet. If your tap water is heavy in sodium, use bottled water for some drinking and the preparation of coffee and tea. It's costly, but the low sodium content can be determined by the labels. Also, artificial sweeteners used in certain diets contain sodium, which also must be compensated for.

Unmasking the Hidden Sources of Sodium

The proper control of sodium intake demands an awareness of the various ways in which sodium can be introduced into the foodstuffs you eat. By mastering the knowledge of sodium sources, you can take a giant step toward anticipating them even before you can verify their existence.

In addition to these hidden sources of sodium, you have to learn what foods contain the most natural quantities of sodium. That doesn't mean you cannot eat them, but you must be aware of the amount of sodium they contain in order to control your intake.

The best way to proceed is to begin a study of foodstuffs with a view to discovering their sodium content. Are they good for you with small sodium quantities, or are they bad for you with large sodium quantities?

By the time I had learned that I was consuming much too much sodium for my bodily needs, I was already in the process of doing something about it. My target area was somewhere between 1,100 and 3,300 milligrams of sodium a day—an average of 2,200, as suggested by the National Research Council of the National Academy of Sciences.

Incidentally, had I been put on a doctor's low-sodium regimen—1,000, 500, or even 250 milligrams of sodium a day—I would have been forced to pay strict attention to my sodium intake. Such regimens become complicated and demand special cooking and tricky food preparation.

WARNING: Such low-sodium diets must be undertaken strictly under the watchful eye of a physician or nutritionist. Because the menus must be somewhat different from the average person's food intake, special care must be taken not to deprive the dieter of *other* essential nutriments. Do *not* undertake any 1,000, 500, or 250 milligram-a-day low-sodium diets on your own. Do so only under the supervision of a doctor or qualified nutritionist.

Tips on Cutting Sodium Intake

Hitting my own target of 2,200 milligrams of sodium a day was not an easy task. So habituated had I become to reaching for the saltcellar—even though I hated salt from the beginning—that I had to do a great deal of rethinking on my general intake of food.

In effect, what I did was simply reorganize my food regimen from top to bottom. I did a kind of culinary housecleaning. This rethinking involved not only what I was actually eating, both at home and dining out, but how to *prepare* food as well.

I've mentioned some of the requirements of a low-sodium intake in passing. However, discovering these facts point by point was a lot harder than simply stumbling over them accidentally. What I learned helped a great deal in reorganizing my thinking on food consumption.

Because my trial-and-error experiments were so complicated—some failing and others succeeding—I won't go into a step-by-step narration of my troubles. Instead, I've tried to organize these discoveries into a kind of random selection of tips to the low-sodium eater as follows:

- Do not use any table salt in cooking.
- Use fresh vegetables rather than processed vegetables whenever you can.
- Add a pinch of sugar to the cooking water in which you are preparing vegetables to help bring out the flavor.
- If you have to use canned vegetables, be sure to purchase low-sodium varieties.
- You can use frozen vegetables, except for some frozen peas, lima beans, and mixed vegetables, which contain sodium as a processing additive. Check the labels.
- If you use prepared vegetable juices, be sure to buy low-sodium varieties.
- Use low-sodium bread and baked goods.
- Don't use regular margarine or butter. Substitute unsalted polyunsaturated margarine. Cook with liquid vegetable oils.
- If you do use butter—and you can if you need to restrict only sodium and not saturated fat and cholesterol—be sure it is unsalted.
- Do not use certain cheeses with high-sodium values: Parmesan, Cheddar, Swiss, or mozzarella. Substitute low-sodium American, low-sodium Cheddar, and low-sodium Swiss cheese, all generally available where you shop. To flavor spaghetti add fennel and coriander.
- Do not use canned soup stocks, bouillon powders, or bouillon cubes. Substitute unsalted homemade soup stocks.
- You can always substitute vinegars and wines for salt in cooking. They are excellent for helping flavor foods.
- Avoid oil-packed tuna and salmon. Substitute water-packed canned tuna and salmon.

- Do not use salt on beef. Flavor it with dry mustard, garlic, marjoram, pepper, sage, or thyme. Or add bay leaf for a fresh, subtle taste. Sprinkle hamburger with lemon juice before broiling. Season meat loaf with chili powder, onions and tomatoes.
- Do not use salt on chicken. Season with curry powder, paprika, parsley, sage, tarragon, thyme, or rosemary.
- Do not use salt on lamb. Rub a little curry powder or turmeric into it, and sprinkle with chopped parsley, mint, rosemary, or turmeric.
- Do not use salt on fresh pork. Try dry mustard, sage, marjoram, thyme, and basil. Try cinnamon and onion on pork chops.
- Do not use salt on veal. Combine crushed bay leaf, curry powder, marjoram, oregano, and powdered ginger, and pound gently into the meat before cooking.
- You can add a flavorful tang to roast pork, veal, and chicken by adding apple slices, pineapple, dried apricots, or cranberries. Sherry is a good addition to these as well.
- Do not use salt on fish. Flavor with bay leaf, fresh sliced lemon, cayenne pepper, curry powder, dill, fennel seed, marjoram, paprika, or thyme.
- Chicken, beef, veal, fish and egg dishes can be flavored by the addition of fresh tomatoes, garlic, and fresh mushrooms.
- Beef, chicken, veal, and lamb can also be flavored by marinating them with salad dressings that include no salt. You can also sprinkle them with lemon juice.
- Do not use salt on salads or in salad dressings. Try chervil, chives, coriander seed, dill, garlic, mint, oregano, or tarragon.
- Do not use salt on vegetables. Add basil, caraway seed, marjoram, savory, dry mustard, or coriander.

- Season carrots with cinnamon or nutmeg.
- Flavor green beans with curry powder, basil, or minced onion.
- Try cinnamon, cloves, dill, ginger, orange or lemon juice and onion with squash.
- Season potatoes with chives and grated onion.
- For soups, stews, and sauces use allspice, basil, mace, marjoram, onion, garlic, sage, or thyme.
- Eggs can be helped along with a sprinkle of curry powder, parsley flakes, chives, pepper, oregano, or paprika. Cloves, cinnamon, and nutmeg also add good flavor.
- Steam vegetables until crisp and tender; the texture is more appealing and flavors as well as nutrients are retained.

Of course, this is just a general list of tips on getting along without salt. You will adjust proportions to your own palate and add to them as you go along. However, it should give you a good working base to select and prepare food that is low in sodium content.

To summarize the main points:

- Remove the saltcellar from the table.
- Avoid the use of table salt or monosodium glutamate in all cooking.
- Avoid all foods that are preserved in brine.
- Avoid all canned vegetables, soups, fish, or prepared dinners, unless marked low-sodium.
- Do not use ketchup, prepared mustard, commercial mayonnaise, soy sauce, or Worcestershire sauce.
- Use only small quantities of high-sodium cheese.
- Avoid all salty snacks like potato chips, pretzels, and salted nuts.

Separating Good from Not So Good

Another particularly effective method for reducing sodium intake became obvious to me when I began investigating the content of sodium in natural and processed food. It was based on the simple fact that some foods have more sodium in them than others. That led me to make up a list with two separate categories, one of foods that were low in sodium and another of foods that were high. It seemed obvious that if I could find enough foods to enjoy in the low-sodium category, I could certainly train myself to get along without overindulging in sodium-saturated foods.

By the very nature of the project I was undertaking, I could certainly make substitutions once in a while, using a high-sodium food if I kept my other intake down to balance it off.

A slightly shortened version of the list I came up with is included in the next chapter.

6

Highs and Lows in Sodium

It is a good idea to remember that you simply cannot completely change your diet and palate overnight. However, by knowing how to substitute certain low-sodium foods for high-sodium foods, you will be able to look forward to a much more salt-free diet. I invite you to make use of the chart I made up for myself.

To help deal with the problem of excess sodium in my diet, I first of all made up a list of foods that had little sodium and a contrasting list of foods that had a lot of sodium. I then set these lists opposite one another to help me make up my mind what to eat. I called one list "good" (low in sodium content) and the other "not so good" (high in sodium content).

I then divided these lists up into a number of separate categories, more for the convenience of comparison than anything else. I started out with baked goods, then went on to beverages, fruits, vegetables, meat and fish, dairy products, soups, spreads, and condiments.

The contrasting lists follow.

Baked Goods

Good	Not So Good
white bread (best if low-sodium)	corn flakes
whole wheat bread (best if low-sodium)	instant oatmeal
some dry cereals	quick-cooking cereals (instant)
cooked cereals	Wheaties
oatmeal	cheese crackers
shredded wheat	cheese bread
plain matzoh	cheese bread
melba toast	soda crackers
some rolls	pizza
rice	corn chips
graham crackers	potato chips
oyster crackers	pretzels
saltines with unsalted tops	salted popcorn

Beverages

Good	Not So Good
alcoholic drinks	chemically softened water
beer	cocktail mixes
carbonated beverages	cocoa mix (if more than 200 mg. sodium per serving)
cocoa mix (if less than 200 mg. sodium per serving)	condensed milk
coffee (black)	tomato juice (salted)
frappes (real milk)	vegetable juice (salted)
milkshakes (real milk)	
orange juice	
tea	
whole or skim milk	

Fruits

Good	Not So Good
canned fruits (in their own juice)	crystallized fruits
	glazed fruits
fresh fruits	preserved fruits
sun-dried fruits	

Vegetables

Good	Not So Good
asparagus (fresh)	cauliflower (frozen in cheese sauce)
beans (dry)	
broccoli	kidney beans (canned or other canned beans not specified as low-sodium)
brussels sprouts	
cabbage	
cauliflower (fresh)	
cauliflower (frozen)	lima beans (frozen)
celery	peas (canned or frozen)
chicory	pickles
corn	potatoes au gratin
cucumbers	instant potatoes
eggplant	sauerkraut
endive	regular canned tomatoes, tomato sauce, tomato paste, tomato puree
escarole	
lettuce	
mushrooms	vegetables, canned
okra	vegetables, mixed (frozen)
onions	vegetables prepared in brine
parsley	
parsnips	
peas (fresh, unsalted)	
peppers	
potatoes (baked or boiled)	
sweet potatoes	

Good	Not So Good
pumpkin (fresh or canned)	
radish	
rice	
soybeans	
summer squash	
winter squash	
tomatoes (fresh or canned if low-sodium)	
canned vegetables (low-sodium)	
vegetable juices (low-sodium)	

Meat and Fish

Good	Not So Good
beef (fresh or frozen	bologna
chicken	cheeseburger
duck	chicken dinner (fast-food)
fish (except shellfish)	fish dinner (frozen)
heart*	frankfurters
kidney*	herring (smoked)
lamb	salmon (canned or smoked)
liver*	
pork	salted fish
salmon (without salt)	salted meats
sweetbreads*	shrimp (canned or fried)
tongue	smoked fish
tuna (packed in water)	smoked meats
turkey	
veal	

*Beware! These are high in cholesterol content.

Dairy Products

Good	Not So Good
American cheese (low-sodium)	American cheese
	blue cheese
Cheddar cheese (low-sodium)	Cheddar cheese
	Meunster cheese
cheese spreads (low-sodium)	cheese spreads
	pasteurized, processed cheeses
cottage cheese (if used in moderation)	Swiss (domestic) cheese
Gruyère, mozzarella, Neufchâtel, and ricotta cheeses and heavy* or light cream (if used in moderation)	
Swiss cheese (low-sodium)	
eggs*	

*Beware! These are high in cholesterol content.

Soups

Good	Not So Good
canned soup (low-sodium)	bouillon cubes
homemade soup	canned soup
	packaged soup mixes

Spreads

Good	Not So Good
butter* (unsalted)	butter (salted)
cream cheese*	dips (commercial)
cream substitute	margarine (salted)
margarine (unsalted)	mayonnaise (regular)
mayonnaise (low-sodium)	mustard (commercial)
peanut butter (unsalted)	olive spread
salad dressings (unsalted)	party spreads
	peanut butter (salted)
	salad dressings (commercial)

*Beware! These are high in cholesterol content.

Condiments

Good	Not So Good
chocolate*	barbecue sauce
garlic powder	garlic salt
gelatin, unflavored	jams (preserved with sodium benzoate)
jams*	
jellies*	jellies (preserved with sodium benzoate)
onion powder	
sugar*	ketchup
	meat sauces and tenderizers
	monosodium glutamate
	salt, table
	onion salt
	soy sauce
	steak sauces
	teriyaki sauce

*If weight control is important, beware of these in excess.

Miscellaneous

Good	Not So Good
baking powder (low-sodium)	baking powder (regular double-acting)
cooking fat* (unsalted)	baking soda
cooking oil (unsalted)	meat drippings (salted)
nuts* (unsalted)	

*If weight control is important, beware of these in excess.

Two Lists of Foods Containing Sodium

Many foods listed in the "not so good" column are actually only moderately high in sodium content. To be fair, I've made up two separate lists—one of foods extremely high in sodium and another of foods moderately high—for you to study.

Foods Extremely High in Sodium

anchovies
bacon
bacon fat
baking powder, baking soda
beef, chipped
beef, corned
bouillon cubes (not salt-free)
caviar
celery salt

cheese (some and excluding low-sodium types)
chili sauce
cod, dried
fish, salted
fish, smoked
frankfurters
garlic salt
herring
ketchup

Foods Extremely High in Sodium (cont.)

luncheon meat
meat extracts
meat sauces
meat tenderizers
meats, salted
meats, smoked
mustard, commercial
nuts, salted
olives
onion salt
pickles

popcorn, salted
potato chips
pretzels
relishes
salt, table
salt pork
sardines
sauerkraut
sausages
soy sauce
Worcestershire sauce

Foods Moderately High in Sodium

beets (canned)
beet greens
beverage mixes
bread
butter, salted
carrots (canned)
celery
clams
crabs
crackers
dandelion greens
fish, canned
kale
kidneys
lobster

margarine, salted
meats, canned
molasses
mustard greens
oysters
rolls
salad dressings,
    commercial
scallops
shrimp
spinach
swiss chard
vegetable juice, canned
vegetables, canned
waffles

Sodium Content in Common Foodstuffs

In controlling sodium intake it is important not to reduce your calcium intake to below 800 milligrams a day and magnesium to below 300 milligrams a day. Unfortunately, many foods high in sodium content are also high in calcium and magnesium content. Calcium and magnesium regulate blood pressure in association with sodium and potassium, and recent studies indicate low levels of these may also contribute to the development of hypertension.

In general, the sodium content of the most common foods you eat follows the principles already explained. However, a long hard look at individual dishes proved to be exceptionally interesting. I was surprised at how much sodium some contained; I was just as surprised at how little others contained.

I made up a list of foods for my own use, determining how many milligrams of sodium were included in one serving of each food item. I used the list to help make up my daily menus.

For your convenience, I've included my selected list here. The figures have been taken from several sources, primarily the U.S. Department of Agriculture's handbook, *Nutritive Value of American Foods* (Agriculture Handbook No. 456). Some figures also came from a Department of Agriculture book, *The Sodium Content of Your Food,* and from other publications, including *Home and Garden Bulletin, No. 233.* In other instances, the sodium content of certain foods was obtained from the label on the container in which the food was purchased.

Serving size became an arbitrary judgment. One pamphlet used a typical serving as 4 ounces; another used 3½ ounces, possibly because 3½ ounces equals 100 grams, and certain nutritional measurements of foods occur in 100-gram lots. Fruits and vegetables selected were usually medium-sized. Soups were considered about 1 cup (8 fluid ounces) per serving.

REMINDER: 1 cup = 8 fluid ounces = ½ pint = 16 tablespoons. 1 gram = 1,000 milligrams. 100 grams = 3.52 ounces. 1 ounce = 28.4 grams.

Sodium Content in Certain Foods

Food	Size of Serving	Milligrams of Sodium
Meats, Fish, and Poultry		
bacon, Canadian	3-ounce slice	537
bacon, regular	2 thick slices	245
beef, lean	3 ounces	55
corned beef	3 ounces	802
ham, cured	3 ounces	795
lamb	3 ounces	58
pork, fresh, lean	3 ounces	59
veal	3 ounces	69
sirloin steak, broiled	3 ounces	67
halibut, broiled with butter	3 ounces	114
herring, smoked	3 ounces	5,234
shrimp, raw	3 ounces	120
shrimp, canned	3 ounces	1,955

Food	Size of Serving	Milligrams of Sodium
chicken, dark meat	4 ounces	100
chicken, drumstick, with skin	1 drumstick	47
chicken, white meat	4 ounces	75
turkey, white meat	4 ounces	93

Processed Meats

bologna	1 slice	260
frankfurter	1 frank	627
salami, beef	1 slice	255

Prepared Dishes

cheeseburger	1 burger	709
hamburger	1 burger	461
pizza, with cheese (14 inch)	1/8 pie	456
pizza, with sausage (14 inch)	1/8 pie	488
chicken pot pie, frozen	1 pie	933

Prepared Meals

beef dinner, frozen	1 dinner	736
chicken dinner, fast-food	1 dinner	2,243
fish dinner, frozen	1 dinner	1,011
turkey dinner, frozen	1 dinner	1,360

Food	Size of Serving	Milligrams of Sodium
Soups		
chicken noodle soup, canned	1 cup	1,020
chicken noodle soup, low-sodium	1 cup	100
chunky beef and vegetable soup, low-sodium	1 cup	75
cream of mushroom soup, canned	1 cup	1,031
tomato soup, low-sodium	1 cup	29
vegetable beef soup, low-sodium	1 cup	51
Vegetables		
artichoke, cooked	1 medium	36
asparagus, cooked	1 spear	1
beans, green, cooked	1 cup	5
beets, cooked	1 cup	73
broccoli, raw	1 stalk	23
broccoli, cooked	1 stalk	18
brussels sprouts, cooked	1 medium	2
cabbage, cooked	1 cup	20
carrots, raw	1 carrot	34
carrots, cooked	1 cup	51
cauliflower, raw	1 cup	13
celery, raw	1 stalk	30
corn, cooked	1 ear	trace

Food	Size of Serving	Milligrams of Sodium
cucumber	7 slices	2
eggplant, cooked	1 cup	2
green peppers, raw	1 large	13
kale, cooked	1 cup	47
lettuce	1 cup	5
lima beans, cooked	1 cup	2
mushrooms	1 cup	11
okra, cooked	10 pods	2
onions, dry	1 medium	10
peas, green, canned	1 cup	401
peas, green, fresh, cooked	1 cup	2
potatoes, baked or broiled	1 potato	5
potatoes au gratin, with cheese	1 cup	1,095
pumpkin, canned	1 cup	5
radish	4 small	2
rutabaga, cooked	1 cup	7
spinach, fresh	1 cup	39
spinach, cooked	1 cup	90
squash, summer, cooked	1 cup	2
squash, winter, baked	1 cup	2
sweet potatoes, baked or broiled	1 potato	15
tomato, raw	1 tomato	4
tomato, cooked	1 cup	10
tomato, canned	1 cup	313
tossed green salad	3 ounces	3
turnips, raw	1 cup	64
turnips, cooked	1 cup	53

Food	Size of Serving	Milligrams of Sodium
Fruits		
fruits, fresh, generally	1 cup	1 to 4
cantaloupe	½ medium	33
fruit cup, fresh	1 cup	2
raisins	1 cup	39
Breads		
biscuits, regular	1 biscuit	175
bread, raisin	1 slice	95
bread, rye	1 slice	139
bread, whole wheat	1 slice	132
bread, whole wheat, low-sodium	1 slice	7
bread, white	1 slice	142
bread, white, low-sodium	1 slice	7
soda crackers	2 crackers	72
crackers, low-sodium	1 cracker	1
crackers, unsalted tops (saltines)	2 crackers	50
Parker House rolls	1 roll	275
pretzel goldfish	10 "fish"	195
graham crackers	2 crackers	94
Ritz crackers	3 crackers	97
matzoh	1 piece	trace
melba toast, unsalted	1 slice	1

Food	Size of Serving	Milligrams of Sodium
Cereals		
corn flakes	1 ounce	256
corn flakes, low-sodium	1¼ cup	10
cream of wheat	¾ cup	2
oatmeal, regular, cooked without salt	1 cup	2
puffed rice	1 cup	1
puffed wheat	1 cup	1
shredded wheat	1 biscuit	1
Cereal Products		
macaroni	1 cup	1
rice, brown	1 cup	10
rice, white	1 cup	6
spaghetti	1 cup	1
Dairy Products		
butter, regular	1 tablespoon	140
butter, unsalted	1 tablespoon	2
buttermilk, cultured	1 cup	319
buttermilk, unsalted	1 cup	122
cheese, American	1 ounce	406
cheese, American, low-sodium	1 ounce	2
cheese, Cheddar	1 ounce	198
cheese, Cheddar, low-sodium	1 ounce	6

Food	Size of Serving	Milligrams of Sodium
cheese, cottage, regular	4 ounces	260
cheese, cottage, unsalted	4 ounces	14
cheese, cottage, low-fat	4 ounces	260
cheese, Muenster	1 ounce	204
cheese, Parmesan, grated	1 ounce	247
cheese, Swiss, natural	1 ounce	201
cheese, Swiss, pasteurized processed	1 ounce	331
eggs, fresh	1 medium	54
cream	1 tablespoon	6
cream, whipping	1 tablespoon	5
margarine	1 tablespoon	140
margarine, unsalted	1 tablespoon	1
milk, whole or skim	1 cup	122
milk, low-fat	1 cup	150
milk, low-sodium	1 cup	6
milk, canned, condensed	1 cup	343
yogurt, plain	8 ounces	106

Beverages

Food	Size of Serving	Milligrams of Sodium
beer	12 ounces	25
dessert wine	3½ ounces	4
gin, rum, vodka, whiskey	1½ ounces	trace
table wine	3½ ounces	5
vermouth	4 ounces	4

Food	Size of Serving	Milligrams of Sodium
coffee	1 cup	2
cola, regular	8 ounces	1
cola, low-calorie	8 ounces	40
fruit juice (orange, grapefruit, apple)	6 ounces	1
pineapple-and-grapefruit drink	8 ounces	80
tea	1 cup	2

Condiments

Food	Size of Serving	Milligrams of Sodium
A-1 sauce	1 tablespoon	275
barbecue sauce	1 tablespoon	130
blue cheese dressing	1 tablespoon	164
ketchup	1 tablespoon	156
ketchup, low-sodium	1 tablespoon	3
French dressing	1 tablespoon	214
French dressing, low-sodium	1 tablespoon	3
mayonnaise	1 tablespoon	89
mayonnaise, low-sodium	1 tablespoon	2
mustard	1 teaspoon	65
Russian dressing	1 tablespoon	138
soy sauce	1 tablespoon	1,319
sweetener	1 packet	5
teriyaki sauce	1 tablespoon	690
tomato sauce, low-sodium	1 tablespoon	50
tomato sauce, regular	½ cup	656
vinegar	1 tablespoon	trace
Worcestershire sauce	1 tablespoon	206

Food	Size of Serving	Milligrams of Sodium
Cooking Aids		
baking powder	1 teaspoon	339
baking powder, low-sodium	1 teaspoon	trace
baking soda	1 teaspoon	821
flour	1 cup	3
garlic salt	1 tablespoon	1,850
meat tenderizer	1 teaspoon	1,750
monosodium glutamate (MSG)	1 tablespoon	492
salt	1 teaspoon	2,132
sugar	1 tablespoon	trace
sugar, brown, packed	1 tablespoon	4
Snacks		
almonds, unsalted, whole	1 cup	5
pickles, dill	1 pickle	928
pickles, dill, low-sodium	1 pickle	5
peanuts, dry-roasted, salted	1 cup	602
peanuts, dry-roasted, unsalted	1 cup	8
peanut butter, regular	1 tablespoon	97
peanut butter, low-sodium	1 tablespoon	1
potato chips	1 large chip	20
pretzels	1 pretzel	101

Food	Size of Serving	Milligrams of Sodium
Desserts		
chocolate chip cookies	2 cookies	69
chocolate pudding, instant	½ cup	161
ginger snaps	4 cookies	161
ice cream, chocolate	1 cup	153
ice cream, French vanilla	1 cup	153
ice cream, vanilla	1 cup	75
milkshake	1 shake	285
pecan pie	⅛ pie	228
tapioca pudding	½ cup	130
Digestive Aids		
Alka-Seltzer	1 tablet	521
Bromo-Seltzer	1 tablet	717
Rolaids	1 tablet	53
Other Medications		
aspirin	2 tablets	49
laxative	1 dose	250
toothpaste	1 brush	trace

7

The Awful Truth: How Much Sodium?

Thinking about low-sodium intake and actually eating food with little sodium in it are two entirely different things. Thinking about avoiding sodium is the dreamer's way of pretending to cut down on sodium intake. Yet I found it necessary to think about foods and their sodium content before I could go about arranging a daily regimen for myself.

I blundered around ineffectually for some time before I got the hang of it. I substituted one thing here and another thing there, trying to eat something that had little sodium content in it instead of something that had a large amount of sodium.

However, I soon realized that I was still eating a large number of foods with sodium content of which I was not really aware. I finally decided I would have to attack the problem with paper and pencil and a hand calculator.

My line of attack is composed of several distinct steps. I list them because they may prove beneficial when you come to your own attack on reckless sodium intake.

1. I made up a list of all the food I ate during the course of a normal day.
2. I then looked up the sodium value for each item.
3. I measured the exact amount of the food that I had eaten or was accustomed to eat.
4. I tried to estimate the exact amount of sodium introduced into the food by cooking. (If I cooked with salt, I simply calculated the amount of sodium as $2/5$ the amount of the salt used.)
5. I checked carefully to find the amount of sodium in each can of food I used, dividing the total amount in the can by the amount I actually ate.
6. I tried to calculate in a similar fashion the amount of sodium involved in preserving foods like cured meats, relishes, salad dressings, and commercial sauces. Containers of such foodstuffs usually listed the amounts of sodium involved.
7. From 2, 3, 4, 5, and 6 above, I calculated the estimated amount of sodium I had ingested. I then tried to see how much sodium I had actually taken in, with my established goal—2,200 milligrams of sodium—always in mind.
8. After going through these steps for several days, I then replaced high-sodium items like processed foods with fresh foods or low-sodium dietetic substitutes.
9. At the same time I was able to cook without using salt at all, replacing it with special herbs and spices.

It's easier to explain if I lead you through the various steps, exactly as I took them.

How Much Sodium Do You Eat Every Day?

Frankly, I was astonished when I toted up my first day's ordinary intake of sodium. There was a great deal more involved than I had thought.

Here was my original breakfast:

pineapple-and-grapefruit drink
corn flakes with milk
white toast
margarine
coffee
milk (for coffee)
sweetener

Thinking about it at first, I assumed there wasn't much sodium in those items at all. None of the foodstuffs *tasted* salty. And yet when I looked up the sodium values for each item, I was appalled:

pineapple-and-grapefruit drink	10 mg. per ounce
corn flakes	256 mg. per ounce
milk	15.25 mg. per ounce
white toast	142 mg. per slice
margarine	140 mg. per tablespoon
coffee	2 mg. per cup
milk (for coffee)	8 mg. per tablespoon
sweetener	5 mg. per packet

I was even more astonished when, in order to determine precisely how much sodium I had consumed, I took step

3 and listed the exact amount of each item of food I had eaten:

pineapple-and-grapefruit drink	6 ounces
corn flakes	1 ounce (1 ounce = 1 cup)
milk	½ cup (4 fluid ounces)
white toast	2 slices
margarine	1 tablespoon
coffee	2 cups
milk (for coffee)	1 tablespoon
sweetener	2 packets

My chart was beginning to take shape. The figures in the last column indicate the amount of sodium I had consumed just for breakfast:

				Mg. of Sodium
pineapple-and-grapefruit drink	6 ounces	×	10	= 60
corn flakes	1 ounce	×	256	= 256
milk	4 fluid ounces	×	15.25	= 61
white toast	2 slices	×	142	= 284
margarine	1 tablespoon	×	140	= 140
coffee	2 cups	×	2	= 4
milk (for coffee)	1 tablespoon	×	8	= 8
sweetener	2 packets	×	5	= 10
				823

I finished calculating only my breakfast, and I had already used up almost one-third of my daily allotment of sodium.

But my lunch was even more sodium-dominated than my breakfast:

		Mg. of Sodium
chicken noodle soup, canned	1 cup	1,020
salami, beef	2 slices	510
whole wheat bread	2 slices	264
mustard	1 teaspoon	65
dill pickle	1 pickle	928
low-calorie cola	8 fluid ounces	40
		2,827

And then of course I listed my predinner refreshment that evening even though I didn't think there was much sodium content in a low-calorie cola—and there isn't. But I forgot that I had pretzels and peanuts along with it.

		Mg. of Sodium
low-calorie cola	12 ounces	60
pretzels	5 pretzels	505
peanuts, salted	4 ounces	301
		866

Note that I had already achieved a sodium intake of 4,516 milligrams without even getting ready to sit down to dinner.

That turned out to be another eye-opener:

		Mg. of Sodium
cream of mushroom soup, canned	1 cup	1,031
ham, cured	3 ounces	795
potatoes au gratin	1 cup	1,095
peas, canned	1 cup	401
tossed green salad	3 ounces	3
French dressing	1 table-spoon	214
pecan pie	1 slice (⅛ pie)	228
coffee	2 cups	4
milk (for coffee)	1 table-spoon	8
sweetener	2 packets	10
		3,789

The awful truth was that on my first day I had consumed over 8 grams of sodium, a grand total of 8,305 milligrams. That was almost four times my target figure. It was obvious that I had to do something about it, and do it right away. I had become a sodium junkie without even enjoying the highs!

Replacing High-Sodium Offenders

The next step was the tricky one—substituting every high-sodium item with a low-sodium substitute. Looking back over my daily menu, I realized that the chief villain behind

the scenes of the drama was the amount of canned, processed, and prepackaged food I had eaten:

	Mg. of Sodium
pineapple-and-grapefruit drink	60
corn flakes	256
chicken noodle soup, canned	1,020
salami, beef	510
mustard	65
dill pickle	928
pretzels	505
peanuts, salted	301
cream of mushroom soup, canned	1,031
ham, cured	795
potatoes au gratin	1,095
peas, canned	401
French dressing	214
pecan pie	228

Basically, the biggest inroads I made into my sodium
intake was in the immediate substitution of fresh fruit, vegetables, and meats for all processed varieties.

Breakfast alone told the story:

Old Breakfast	New Breakfast	Portion Old/New	Milligrams of Sodium	
			Old	New
pineapple-and-grapefruit drink	*fresh orange juice*	6 ounces	60	*1*
corn flakes	*shredded wheat*	1 cup/ 2 biscuits	256	*2*
milk	*milk*	½ cup	61	*61*
white toast	*bread, low-sodium*	2 slices/1 slice	284	*7*
margarine	*margarine, salt-free*	1 tbs.	140	*1*
coffee	*coffee*	2 cups	4	*4*
milk (for coffee)	*milk, low-sodium*	1 tbs.	8	*0*
sweetener	*sweetener, low-sodium*	2 packets	10	*0*
			823	76

Lunch wasn't really very hard either.

Old Lunch	New Lunch	Portion Old/New	Milligrams of Sodium	
			Old	New
chicken noodle soup, canned	*tomato soup, low-sodium, made with water*	1 cup/½ cup	1,020	*15*
salami, beef	*chicken, white meat*	2 slices (3 ounces)	510	*56*
whole wheat bread	*whole wheat bread, low-sodium*	2 slices	264	*14*
mustard	*lettuce*	1 tsp./2 leaves	65	*2*
dill pickle	*dill pickle, low-sodium*	1 pickle	928	*5*
low-calorie cola	*cola, regular*	8 fluid ounces	40	*1*
			2,827	93

Old Snack	New Snack	Portion Old/New	Milligrams of Sodium	
			Old	New
low-calorie cola	*fresh fruit juice*	12 ounces/ *6 ounces*	60	*1*
pretzels	–	5 pretzels	505	–
peanuts, salted	*almonds, unsalted*	4 ounces/ *1 cup*	301	*5*
			866	6

Old Dinner	New Dinner	Portion Old/New	Milligrams of Sodium	
			Old	New
cream of mushroom soup, canned	*vegetable beef soup, low-sodium*	1 cup	1,031	*51*
ham, cured	*sirloin steak, broiled*	3 ounces	795	67
potatoes au gratin	*potato, baked*	1 cup/ *1 potato*	1,095	*5*
peas, canned	*peas, freshly cooked*	1 cup	401	*2*
tossed green salad	*tossed green salad*	3 ounces	3	*3*
French dressing	*French dressing, low-sodium*	1 tbs.	214	*3*
pecan pie	*fruit cup, fresh*	1 slice/1 cup	228	*2*
coffee	*coffee*	2 cups	4	*4*
milk (for coffee)	*milk*	1 tbs.	8	*8*
sweetener	*sweetener, low-sodium*	2 packets	10	*0*
			3,789	145

A grand total for the new menu of 320 milligrams of sodium for the day!

8

Seven Days of Salt-Free Eating

I discovered early on that it was really not enough simply to keep good thoughts about avoiding sodium. It was necessary to develop a plan of action and then play it out like a war game. Without some kind of scenario, it was impossible to determine how much sodium I was actually eating.

After totaling my sodium intake for one day, as detailed in the previous chapter, I finally decided I had to take myself in hand and determine ahead of time exactly what I was going to eat each day and stick to the plan. In other words, I put myself on a rigorous schedule. It was easy enough to do—I simply used the same steps I had used to determine what my sodium intake was and made up a daily chart of my food for the week accordingly.

When I did that, I discovered that there were certain rules of thumb I could follow so that later on I didn't really need to write it all down ahead of time. I got used to the idea of what I could eat and what I should stay away from.

If I overindulged one day, I could then balance that off with a slightly more restricted diet.

I also wanted to make sure I wasn't ignoring completely my caloric intake; the plan I evolved was to cut down on sodium *and* calories at the same time. Generally speaking, there were several guidelines I followed in trying to put together appetizing meals for myself and still stay within the restrictions I had arbitrarily set up.

What to Eat for Breakfast

Breakfast seemed fairly easy. I didn't take the crash dieter's way out and confine myself to coffee. Frankly, I always needed something in my stomach or I tended to overeat at lunch and dinner. So I tried to take some nourishment with low-sodium products.

To begin, I used either fresh fruit or fruit juice. Naturally, freshly squeezed orange juice or a fresh grapefruit were the best. But I couldn't always count on getting either. When I couldn't get fresh fruit, I used frozen. Actually, I could have used canned as well. Most fruit juices don't have too much sodium in them no matter how they are processed. Canned fruit juice tends to have a slightly different taste to it; that was my only complaint.

As for cereals, I knew that there were low-sodium dry cereals and cooked cereals. But I found that most cooked cereals were low enough in sodium not to cause any big change in my eating habits. Sometimes in the summer I balanced out cooked cereals with dry cereals. These tended to contain more sodium, but there were always certain substitutes I could use if I felt I was getting too much.

I didn't eat much more than juice, cereal, toast, and coffee for breakfast most of the week, but on weekends I would usually have bacon and eggs, pancakes or waffles. I found that pancakes and bacon add a stiff amount to my sodium intake, and decided to keep them down to once or perhaps twice a week if my sodium count could take it. Actually, my original eating habits had been about right to begin with.

If I ate breakfast out, I found that I could eat just about what I was used to. The only thing I learned to look out for were scrambled eggs and fried eggs. Most of the time they were prepared with salt and salted butter. For toast, I found I liked low-sodium bread, but it was more costly than regular bread. If my numbers worked out all right, I usually stuck with thin slices of regular bread.

What to Eat for Lunch

Even lunch seemed somewhat routine. I was in the habit of building my luncheon menu around some kind of sandwich. Although I used to prefer hamburgers, I finally gave them up because the quality of the meat served in restaurants and fast-food chains has declined so dramatically. Much of the meat seems extremely greasy and sometimes even watery. My favorite type of lunch sandwich became that made from leftovers like sliced turkey, sliced chicken, sliced meat loaf, and egg salad. I deliberately kept away from cheeses, although I knew there were low-sodium varieties obtainable.

As a preliminary to the sandwich, I usually drank some kind of fruit juice in the summer and spring months, such as pineapple juice or grape juice. Sometimes, to vary that appetizer, I would eat some fruit—fresh, canned or frozen. In the winter months, I would substitute soup for the fruit juice. When I decided on restricting my sodium diet, I simply made my own soup or selected low-sodium canned soups.

Salads proved to be no problem. The catch was in the salad dressing. Usually I had doused my lettuce or tossed greens with French dressing. But commercially prepared French dressing proved to be a villain in the sodium picture. I cut it out entirely. There were many substitutes. However, once I began to experiment, I realized that the taste of lettuce itself was not all that bad even *without* seasoning!

As for tossed green salad, it's just as good without commercially prepared dressing as with it. However, if you can't stand to eat salads without some kind of disguise, there are plenty of substitutes you can prepare with herbs and spices. I've included information on them in Chapters Eleven and Twelve.

Of course, to vary the sandwich routine, I sometimes ate a hot dish. Whenever I substituted, I made sure I was using low-sodium meat, poultry, fish, and vegetables. It proved to be not too much of a problem.

For dessert I found that ice cream, cakes, cookies, and fresh, canned, or frozen fruits were all on my checklist, except that I made sure when I bought gelatins, puddings, cakes, and cookies to get the low-sodium varieties.

What to Eat for Dinner

Dinner proved to be the most crucial meal of all, as might be expected. It was here that I was able to work out in detail the proper balance for the day. That is, if I happened to entertain a client at lunch and took in a little too much sodium, I could then balance that out with a very low-sodium dinner at home. Also, with the use of spices and herbs to season the food cooked at home, the sodium intake could be cut down to the bare minimum if necessary.

There were really no preconceived rules when it came to dinner. Each day was a special case in itself. Main courses could be meat of a variety of types, fish of many kinds, poultry perhaps, or even casseroles or preparations of chili, spaghetti, or other mixed concoctions. The variety was endless.

The Joys of Snacking

Snacking is an integral part of the Great American Dream, a handful of cheese nips here, a pile of salted peanuts there, ad infinitum. Because most snacks—including cheese products—tend to be foodstuffs preserved rather than prepared and served fresh, the sodium content is usually higher than in regular foods.

The perfect solution to snacking is to cut it down to a bare minimum, particularly if you want to decrease your sodium intake as well as your caloric intake. However, if you can't stand the thought of not munching on something at odd hours, make sure that you confine yourself to unsalted nuts, low-sodium snacks, and fresh fruits and vegetables, when possible.

To give you an example of what I mean, I've compiled a random assortment of sample breakfasts, lunches, and dinners. I've also included a sodium count as accurate as possible for each menu.

Because it's easier to cook your own special low-sodium dishes than to depend on processed food, I've included some special home preparations in these menus; recipes are given in Chapter Fifteen. (Each food for which a recipe is provided is marked with an asterisk in the following group of sample menus.)

This assorted group of sample menus is in no way intended to be a rigid dietary regimen. I've included it to give you an idea of how you can make up your own menus. The sodium counts are quite low in some cases; you can use one meal at random to balance out an otherwise high-sodium day.

You will note that if you were to put yourself on a diet consisting of these sample meals, you would find your sodium intake a great deal lower than the daily average of 2,200 milligrams recommended by the National Research Council of the National Academy of Sciences. Consequently, there's no reason you can't substitute a higher-sodium item in any one of these meals if you want.

NOTE: Recipes for all dishes with asterisks in front of them are given in Chapter Fifteen.

Samples of Low-Salt Breakfasts

		Mg. of Sodium
orange juice, fresh or frozen	4 ounces	1
Maltex, cooked without salt	½ cup	3
milk	½ cup	61
*nut bread	1 slice	16
margarine, unsalted	1 tablespoon	1
marmalade	1 tablespoon	3
coffee or tea	1 cup	2
		87 mg.

		Mg. of Sodium
grapefruit	½ medium	1
egg, soft-boiled	1 egg	59
*savory shaker	1 teaspoon	trace
toast, whole wheat, low-sodium	2 slices	14
margarine, unsalted	1 tablespoon	1
strawberry jam	1 tablespoon	2
coffee or tea	1 cup	2
		79 mg.

cantaloupe	¼ melon	12
shredded wheat	2 biscuits	2
strawberries, fresh or frozen	½ cup	1
milk	½ cup	61
melba toast, unsalted	1 slice	1
raspberry jam	1 tablespoon	2
coffee or tea	1 cup	2
		81 mg.

pineapple juice, frozen	4 ounces	1
French toast, low-sodium	2 slices	73
margarine, unsalted	1 tablespoon	1
*raspberry sauce	¼ cup	2
coffee or tea	1 cup	2
		79 mg.

		Mg. of Sodium
orange sections, fresh	1 orange	1
oatmeal, no salt added	¾ cup	1
sliced walnuts	1 tablespoon	trace
brown sugar	2 tablespoons	8
grated nutmeg	⅛ teaspoon	trace
milk	½ cup	61
coffee or tea	1 cup	2
		73 mg.

grapefruit	½ medium	1
milk	1 tablespoon	8
egg, scrambled in 1 teaspoon margarine	1 egg	59
*savory shaker	1 teaspoon	trace
toast, white, low-sodium	1 slice	7
margarine, unsalted	1 tablespoon	1
marmalade	1 tablespoon	3
coffee or tea	1 cup	2
		81 mg.

grapefruit juice, frozen	4 ounces	1
Cream of Wheat	¾ cup	2
apple, chopped	½ apple	1
cinnamon	sprinkle	trace
milk	½ cup	61
toast, white, low-sodium	2 slices	14

		Mg. of Sodium
margarine, unsalted	1 tablespoon	1
coffee or tea	1 cup	2
		82 mg.

Samples of Low-Salt Lunches

		Mg. of Sodium
vegetable-beef soup, low-sodium	1 cup	51
*egg salad sandwich filling	1 sandwich	61
fresh sliced tomato	2 slices	1
bread, white, low-sodium	2 slices	14
carrot curls	3 slices	trace
apple, fresh	1 apple	2
coffee or tea	1 cup	2
		131 mg.

tomato soup, low-sodium	1 cup	29
*spinach and mushroom salad	1 serving	112
*zesty shaker	1 teaspoon	1
melba toast, unsalted	2 slices	2
macaroon	1 cookie	7
coffee or tea	1 cup	2
		153 mg.

		Mg. of Sodium
beefburger, home-broiled	4 ounces	65
tomato, sliced	2 slices	1
lettuce	2 leaves	2
French fries, frozen, no salt added	3 ounces	4
*spicy shaker	1 teaspoon	1
pear, fresh	1 pear	2
cranapple juice with fresh mint	1 cup	6
		81 mg.

*chicken salad on lettuce leaves	1 serving	111
*nut bread	2 slices	32
margarine, unsalted	1 tablespoon	1
orange sherbet	½ cup	10
tea, iced, with lime wedge	1 cup	2
		156 mg.

*baked macédoine	1 serving	56
lettuce, romaine	4 ounces	3
*French dressing, low-sodium	1 tablespoon	3
fresh fruit cup, chilled	½ cup	1
coffee, iced	1 cup	2
		65 mg.

		Mg. of Sodium
fresh tomato and chive omelet	1 egg, ½ tomato	61
tossed green salad	4 ounces	4
oil and vinegar dressing (no salt added)	1 tablespoon	1
plain soft roll	1 roll	90
margarine, unsalted	1 tablespoon	1
apple, baked	1 apple	2
tea	1 cup	2
		161 mg.
sliced turkey breast sandwich	2 ounces	47
(bread, white, low-sodium)	2 slices	14
*fresh herbal shaker of choice	1 teaspoon	trace to 1
mayonnaise, low-sodium	1 tablespoon	2
*cole slaw (vinegar, oil, shaker)	⅔ cup	20
lemon ice	½ cup	0
cola drink	8 ounces	1
		85 mg.

Samples of Low-Salt Dinners

		Mg. of Sodium
*chicken breasts in white wine sauce	1 serving (6 ounces)	95
broccoli, steamed, with lemon squeezed over	3 stalks	54
potato, baked	1 potato	5
*herb margarine	1 tablespoon	1
orange sections with shredded coconut (2 tablespoons)	½ cup	4
		159 mg.
*Western tamale pie	1 serving	151
tossed green salad	4 ounces	4
*French dressing, low-sodium	1 tablespoon	3
fresh strawberries	8-10	1
with banana	1 banana	1
coffee or tea	1 cup	2
		162 mg.
*shish kebab	1 serving	116
steamed rice sprinkled with crushed thyme	1 cup	6 / 0
tossed green salad with	4 ounces	4
vinegar and oil dressing	4 ounces	4
*apple brown betty	1 serving	24
coffee or tea	1 cup	2
		156 mg.

		Mg. of Sodium
*baked flounder fillets	1 serving	174
potato, boiled, with parsley	1 potato	5
steamed green beans with	1 cup	5
unsalted butter	1 tablespoon	2
and rosemary		0
*cucumber salad	7 slices	4
*sunshine cake	1 serving	28
coffee or tea	1 cup	2
		220 mg.

*saucy baked pork chops	1 serving	85
*spinach surprise	1/4 cup	25
*apple-berry crunch	1 serving	51
coffee or tea	1 cup	2
		163 mg.

*broiled fish fillets with sliced broiled potatoes and broiled tomatoes	1 serving	120
carrots, tiny, steamed	1 serving (2/3 cup)	34
*herb margarine	1 tablespoon	1
leaf lettuce with	1/2 cup	2
oil and vinegar		trace
*lemon custard pudding	1 serving	76
coffee or tea	1 cup	2
		235 mg.

		Mg. of Sodium
*lamb curry	1 serving	100
rice, brown	1 cup	10
(add pinch of nutmeg & cloves to rice)		0
salad of avocado,	1 avocado	9
orange, and	1 orange	1
watercress	1 serving	55
*pears, baked	1 serving	2
coffee or tea	1 cup	2
		179 mg.

9

Shopping the Salt–Free Way

Since the discovery that sodium can be harmful to the potential hypertensive, food manufacturers have begun to devise ways of limiting the amount of sodium used in preserving and in seasoning foodstuffs. When I began looking around for products with low-sodium contents, I could not find many that were particularly tasty.

Nor had the food industry then devised ways and means of providing substitutes for ordinary cooking elements that contain sodium, for example, baking powder and baking soda. Now all that is changed. Low-sodium shopping has become a way of life for many. Most products that once were high in sodium are now available in low-sodium forms. You have to read the labels carefully to learn how much sodium is in each container.

One of the discoveries I made when I was first searching for the proper items for a balanced diet that included low-sodium foods was the importance of potassium in foodstuffs. I mentioned in Chapter Four that the sodium to potassium balance is extremely important in the human body in order to control the size of the arteries and that foods high in potassium are generally considered better for the hypertensive than foods high in sodium.

However, in restricting sodium in a diet, the amount of potassium may also be reduced to below the minimum standard. Many diets low in sodium may cut out foods that are high in sodium and in potassium. By eliminating *too many* foods that have sodium (and potassium), the potassium content may be lowered considerably. A good low-sodium diet must continue to provide enough potassium to keep the body's balance correct.

Another problem is that food processing and the use of spicy seasonings tend to upset the natural balance between these two most important chemical elements.

The Magic of Potassium

With that point learned, I began to pay attention to my potassium intake. In general, many fruits and vegetables contain potassium. Beneficial for potassium content are bananas, plums, figs, oranges, grapefruit, prunes, raisins, apricots, nectarines, melon, broccoli, cabbage, brussels sprouts, potatoes, winter squash, and tomatoes. Fruits should be fresh, sun-dried, or canned salt-free. The vegetables should be fresh, frozen without salt, or canned low-sodium with enough potassium for the average person.

In cooking, however, the substitution of potassium for sodium in certain ingredients is one of the most important alterations to remember. For example, baking soda is a fabulous cooking aid. Without it you would not be able to bake. Yet one teaspoon of baking soda contains 821 milligrams of sodium!

However, potassium bicarbonate can be substituted for baking soda and will perform all the things baking soda (sodium bicarbonate) does. One teaspoon of potassium bicarbonate contains almost no sodium.

As for baking powder, a teaspoon of it contains 339 milligrams of sodium. A low-sodium baking powder that has been developed contains only a trace of sodium per teaspoon. Regular milk contains about 500 milligrams of sodium to the quart. Low-sodium milk, sold in powdered form, contains only 25 to 50 milligrams per quart but is extremely unpalatable. Regular margarine contains approximately 50 milligrams to the teaspoon. Low-sodium margarine contains only 1 milligram to the tablespoon.

These are a few highlights only. Let's take up these points one by one, with a little more basic information.

Low-Sodium Baking Powder

You can purchase low-sodium baking powder at most supermarkets. Actually, baking powder is simply a combination of various ingredients mixed together to cause dough to rise in baking.

One such mixture includes corn starch, sodium bicarbonate, calcium acid phosphate, and sodium aluminum sulphate. Note that two of those ingredients contain sodium. However, both of those sodium-containing ingredients can be withdrawn and potassium-containing ingredients substituted.

In cooking with potassium-type baking powder, you must increase the amount of powder used, making it one-half again as much as the recipe calls for. That is, if the recipe requires 1 teaspoon of baking powder, use 1½ teaspoons of potassium-type baking powder. If you buy a commercially available substitute for baking powder, be sure to follow the directions on the package.

Low-Sodium Baking Soda: Potassium Bicarbonate

As for low-sodium baking soda, simply substitute potassium bicarbonate on your shopping list. When cooking with it, use exactly the same amount of potassium bicarbonate as is called for in the recipe for ordinary baking soda.

Milk and Cream

Most milk is high in sodium content—regular, skimmed, low-fat, certified, condensed, powdered, and evaporated. There are, however, several brands of low-sodium milk now on the market. Unfortunately they are not readily accepted because of their taste. Both regular and low-sodium milk are sold in powdered form. Low-sodium milk contains only about one-fifteenth as much sodium as regular milk does.

Cream contains almost no sodium. Only 6 milligrams of sodium occur in a tablespoon of cream. Cream should be used sparingly if weight loss and fat reduction in your diet are important. Do not use cream substitutes; they may contain sodium.

WARNING: Do not be perturbed at reading on a container of pure cream that it contains sodium alginate. The chemical is a preservative, and it contains sodium. However, in fresh cream, only .001 parts of sodium alginate is used to 1 part of cream.

Chocolate

Oddly enough, most chocolate-base cocoas contain about 17 milligrams of sodium to a teaspoon. However, Hershey's cocoa contains almost none at all—less than 1 milligram to the measure. In general, cocoa is not recommended but if you are watching your sodium intake and you must have cocoa, be sure to specify Hershey brand cocoa.

Salt-Free Margarine

Look for salt-free margarine in the *freezer section* of the supermarket. Salt-free margarine must be kept frozen in your own refrigerator after you buy it. Remove only the stick you are using and keep it in the regular part of the refrigerator.

Salt Substitutes

There are a number of salt substitutes for sale now. Check them over carefully before buying. One "low-salt" substitute contains at least half the sodium content of regular salt. The best way to avoid using salt in cooking is to forget about it entirely and substitute herbs, spices, vinegar, or dry table wines. Even lemon juice will add the right flavor to food you used to season heavily with salt.

Cereals

Hot cereals generally contain less sodium than dry cereals, although there are exceptions. Uncooked hot cereals that come in bulk and require some time to cook are usually low in sodium. Instant cereals that need only the addition of hot water to cook probably have salt added to make them quick-cook. Be sure to check all labels before buying. Bulk cereals contain 5 or less milligrams of sodium per serving. However, quick-cook cereals and specially flavored types contain from 250 to 350 milligrams per serving.

Cold cereals (dry cereals) contain varying amounts of sodium—some about 150 milligrams per serving, others as high as 485 milligrams per one-ounce serving. Check labels to find out how much sodium each brand contains. For example, all dry bran cereal contains 485 milligrams of sodium per one-ounce serving; puffed wheat contains 5 or less per cup. Raw, unprocessed bran contains only a trace of sodium.

Bacon Substitute

A hickory-smoked yeast powder can be used as a substitute for the flavor of bacon to make eggs taste better. It comes in powdered form which you can sprinkle on or mix into any recipe you want. Usually this type of flavoring is sold at health food outlets, but it can also be found in some supermarkets.

Syrups

Molasses, one of the most popular types of syrup used in cooking, is moderately high in sodium. Other syrups, like real maple syrup, contain very little. However, maple-*flavored* syrup has a lot of sodium in it.

NOTE: Honey has *no* sodium in it at all.

Condiments

Commercial mixtures like chili sauce, ketchup, mustard, Worcestershire sauce, and others contain a great deal of sodium, usually both to season and to preserve. However, most of the manufacturers of commercial condiments now produce low-sodium varieties of their popular flavors. Be sure to check the labels for specifics.

Peanut Butter

Peanut butter contains about 100 or more milligrams of sodium for every 2 tablespoons—considered an average serving, for example, to make a sandwich. However, there are specific brands that contain extremely low amounts of sodium. Look on the labels for the amount of sodium per serving. Low-sodium peanut butter usually contains about 15 milligrams for each 1 tablespoon-size serving.

Bread

The production of bread with a low-sodium content causes one problem in its storage and marketing. Salt is used as a preservative. Baked goods that contain little sodium must be stored and sold from refrigerated sections of the store. If you buy low-sodium bread, you must keep it in the freezer section of your refrigerator or it will spoil quickly. Be sure to purchase "salt-free water-based" bread, not just "milk-based" bread. Avoid breads that are made with baking soda and regular baking powder. Of course, if you make these breads yourself, you should substitute potassium ingredients for the sodium ingredients.

Container Labels

At present there are no regulations to define low-sodium foods. Instead they are labeled in a number of different ways, using such terms as "salt-controlled," "salt-reduced," "salt-free," and "low-sodium" designations. All these catch-words really mean the same thing: The sodium quantity is *controlled*, not *avoided*.

If the label states the number of milligrams of sodium in the package, be sure to compute the milligrams per serving and not that of the entire contents. The reverse is true too. Sodium content per serving can be tricky. If a can of soup serves four and contains 800 milligrams per serving, the entire can contains 3,200 milligrams. If you divide the can into two servings, rather than four, you will get 1,600 milligrams apiece, rather than the 800 per serving the can specifies. I am not saying that the labels are deceiving. I am simply saying that you should study them carefully to find out how much you will be getting in the serving you eat.

Many labels do not contain specific amounts of sodium but do list ingredients. Watch out for words like salt, sodium, monosodium glutamate (MSG), leavening (baking powder), soda (baking soda), milk, milk powder, nonfat milk solids, and preservatives that contain sodium.

NOTE: There are two exceptions to these "danger" words: sodium alginate in fresh cream and ascorbic acid used to preserve fresh fruits and juices. They are used in such scanty amounts that they are usually harmless.

Serving Measurements

Be sure to note the difference between 2 mg. and 2 g. The symbol *mg* means milligram. The symbol *g* means gram. There are 1,000 milligrams in one gram. A milligram is $\frac{1}{1000}$ of a gram. There are also various ways of defining a "serving" on cans and containers. Some dry cereals are measured in ounces. That means dry ounces as opposed to fluid ounces. The confusion is exacerbated by the fact that 1 cup contains 8 fluid ounces. However, a serving of brewed coffee is measured in portions of 6 fluid ounces per cup. Coffee in the can is measured in dry ounces; one dry ounce equals 28 grams.

Other measures are equally confusing. One teaspoon equals $1/6$ fluid ounce. One tablespoon equals $1/2$ fluid ounce. One fluid ounce equals $1/8$ cup. Four fluid ounces equals $1/2$ cup, and so on. 2 cups equals 1 pint, and 4 cups, 1 quart.

Dietetic Foods

Certain foods are canned, packaged, or frozen with limited quantities of salt, sodium preservatives, or sugar to help people on reducing, diabetic, or allergy diets. However, these foods may contain ingredients saturated with sodium, enough of it to disrupt the low-sodium regimen. Even items labeled as low sodium may contain too much for your use. Be sure to understand the quantities mentioned. Choose the item with the lowest sodium count.

Cheeses

Generally speaking, cheese is high in natural sodium. For that reason it is not recommended for anyone on a low-sodium diet. However, there are low-sodium cheeses and others with moderate amounts of sodium available.

For some tastes, low-sodium cheese is much too bland for the palate. However, you can always add spices and herbs to make it more tasty.

10

Cooking the Salt-Free Way

One teaspoon of table salt thrown into a pot of boiling vegetables contains about 2,100 milligrams of sodium—nearly a day's intake of an entirely adequate and moderate 2,200 milligrams.

The moral is obvious. In addition to putting the saltcellar back in the cupboard, the second most obvious way to cut down on sodium intake is in the kitchen hovering over the stove.

However, modern cooks and chefs have always relied a great deal on the magic of salt to enhance certain subtle flavors in foodstuffs. The power of salt to heighten the esoteric flavors within food is its greatest culinary asset. It is even true in making candy—a pinch of salt is used to bring out the candy's characteristic best taste. Salt also brings out certain flavors in uncooked food, as when sprinkled on citrus fruits.

I was making war on salt, and in the spirit of a military

briefing, I thought it best to know my enemy before settling down to try to attack and conquer. And so I drew up a brief on salt's strong points—the real reasons it had become so formidable an adversary in the kitchen. It would be a preliminary evaluation that would shape my thinking when I began my campaign against sodium.

How Salt Seasons Food

When used in cooking, salt improves the taste, appearance, and consistency of food in various ways:

- When added to the water in which a vegetable is cooked, salt tends to dehydrate the vegetable, drawing away any excess moisture and leaving the food firmer and thus easier to eat.
- When salt is used in the cooking process with meats and fish, it dehydrates them as well, drawing excess moisture out of the food itself and leaving it more solid and drier.
- When used in cooking hot cereals, salt tends to cut down the absorption of water by the grain itself and helps firm up each piece of grain for better eating.
- When used in the water in which an egg is boiled, salt helps give toughness and strength to the egg, which might more easily fall apart without salt.
- When used in making bread, salt helps keep bread fresh for a longer time. However, it may inhibit the growth of yeast and adversely affect the formation of gluten if it is not used properly.
- When used with soups, stews, stocks, and sauces, salt brings out and clarifies the taste if added in small quantities early in the cooking process.

- When added during cooking—not after—salt most effectively brings out the flavoring of the food and adds a seasoning to any flavor.

Because of salt's various properties, it long ago became surrounded by a mystique which tended to give it a magical power in cookery. At that time, of course, no one really knew that salt had properties that could be harmful to certain people who might use it to excess.

Other Seasonings That Intensify Flavor

Along with salt, pepper became the number two seasoner, usually sharing a place of honor alongside the saltcellar in the modern home. Pepper is only one of literally scores of other seasonings. These substitutes for salt and pepper generally break down into two of three different kinds of flavor intensifiers: herbs and spices. More recently, especially as a substitute in cooking, lemon juice has been added as a separate and successful alternative to salt.

Even a palate that has become habituated and addicted to the flavor of salt can be wooed, tempted and seduced by the use of some of the many enticers available. I determined from the beginning to use all that I could to help put down the potential killer I had discovered on my dining room table.

Here are the big three, briefly:

- An herb is usually the leaf of an aromatic or savory plant valued for its use as a special seasoning. Generally it comes from a seed-producing annual, biennial, or perennial that does not develop persistent canes but dies down at the end of each season.

- A spice is the seed, stem, leaf, root, shoot, fruit, or blossom of a plant, usually crushed to provide specific flavors to enhance the taste of food. Spices can come from bushes, shrubs, and trees of any shape or size.
- Lemon juice is only one of several juices of citrus fruits, many of which can be used to add zest to most foods. Citrus juice can act alone or in combination with herbs, thus doubling the enjoyment of flavor.

Each herb and spice has an affinity to certain special foods. Not every herb or spice can go indiscriminately with any meat, poultry or fish dish. Some work well together; others do not. It is best to know the particular qualities and abilities of each herb and spice before you use it.

All About Herbs

With rare exceptions, the best herb is the fresh herb. Most herbs can be purchased in dried state too, but not one of them will taste quite so good as one grown fresh. Most of the important herbs can be grown easily in a small, sunny plot. Chervil and summer savory are unfortunately much less savory when they are used dried; they are far superior in their fresh state. Other important herbs—basil, chives, parsley, and tarragon—are never really as good in their dried form as they are in their fresh form. Even sage, which is good in its dried form, is better fresh.

You can use a small garden plot to grow herbs, or you can set out small pots in the backyard, or the patio, or even on the window sill. It is not within the parameters of this book to go into an extensive study of herb growing, but I can state that there are several important considerations in the cultivation of herbs:

* Most varieties of herbs require plenty of sunlight.
* Most herbs need constant attention. They have a tendency to sprawl and need regimentation.
* Herbs need pruning in order to force fresh leaves to form.
* The growth of herbs needs proper drainage. They seem to prefer dry and sunny places.
* Most herbs grow better and provide better flavor if they can be grown out-of-doors, although hothouse plants do produce good-flavored leaves.
* Herbs should be grown where they will not be sprayed or subject to dogs.
* When drying herbs, store them in tightly covered, light-proof jars in a dark, cool place.
* If insects appear on the herbs, strip the leaves and throw them away.

Although a fresh herb always provides a better and more subtle final flavor, a dried herb usually provides three to four times the intensity of flavor of a fresh herb. For this reason, it is best when using a fresh herb in cooking to put in about three or four times as much as the dried-herb requirement. Note that the effectiveness of a homegrown herb, whether dried or fresh, is far superior to an herb bought commercially.

Here are a few tips on preparing herbs for use in cooking:

* Dried herbs retain their flavor best if pulverized before using.
* To reconstitute dried herbs and develop their flavors, soak them in water, stock, milk, lemon juice, wine, olive

oil, or vinegar—anything you can incorporate into the recipe. Soak for ten minutes to one hour before using.
- Place nonpowdered dried herbs in a cloth bag, or a stainless metal tea ball, for easy removal during cooking.
- To freeze herbs, parboil them for ten seconds, and then plunge them into ice water for one minute. Dry out between towels, and store the leaves in small, airtight plastic bags or containers. Put them in the freezing compartment until you use them.

Every herb has a special characteristic or characteristics and can be used with certain other herbs and spices. Each has a specific kind of food with which it is the most compatible for maximum advantage. See the next chapter for a list of the main herbs, along with specific tastes or uses, and a recommended type of food to use each with.

All About Spices

It's not hard to confuse spices with herbs, but the difference is an obvious one. An herb is pretty much served as the leaf of a small plant—either dried or fresh. A spice is usually a ground-up or crushed part of a plant. An herb can be used in quantity. A spice is usually used sparingly. Rarely is a spice used fresh. An herb can be used fresh or dried.

The use of spices dates back to the Middle Ages, even before salt became the household item it is today. The privilege of eating delicately seasoned foods was specifically reserved for the aristocrats and courtiers around the palace of the king. Most of the spices used came from the Orient. One reason Marco Polo traveled to China was to open up trade routes to bring spices and silks back to the Mediterranean people.

Naturally, spices were used to preserve as well as season food. Lacking that ability, the Mediterranean peoples found themselves eating unpalatable foods and longing for well-flavored, edible foodstuffs. Not only was Marco Polo's trip to China one result of this demand for spices, but Columbus's trip westward to seek a passage to the Orient resulted from a need to open up trade routes for spices and condiments.

Today spices generally remind us of far-off places: bay leaves are reminiscent of Turkish cuisine; cinnamon of Sri Lanka perhaps; red-hot peppers of Mexico.

Here are some tips on using spices in cooking:

- It is a good idea to purchase a spice from a reliable merchant. Although the quantity of spice you use is small, its use has a great effect on the food flavored. Only the best should be allowed to enhance your food.
- Keep an eye on your spice shelf. Ground spices should be replenished at least once a year. A spice tends to lose strength rapidly. A good way to prevent spoilage or wastage is to mark each spice container with the date of purchase.
- Store spices in containers that are tightly covered and resist moisture. Keep them in a cool, dark place.
- When cooking with spices, roll them up in a cloth or place them in a stainless metal tea ball. Remove them from the pot when you have finished cooking the dish to be flavored.
- Avoid overboiling certain spices since they become bitter and may scorch easily.
- When cooking with spices, learn how to spice to taste

rather than to measure. The cook's subtle taste determines the final flavor of the food.

WARNING: If you use a spice in a foodstuff you intend to freeze and keep awhile before using, remember that spices do not hold up well when stored for any length of time.

The same advice given about herbs applies to spices as well: each has a special characteristic or characteristics. Each can be used with other herbs and spices. It is mandatory that you know what kinds of spices to use with specific types of main dishes and courses. In Chapter Twelve there is a list of important spices, along with specific tastes and uses and a recommended type of food to use each with.

All About Lemon Juice

The use of lemon juice as a substitute for salt is not in any way new, but its use has increased recently because of the continuing news about the harmful effects of sodium in certain individual diets.

Here are some tips you can use in cooking with lemon juice as a salt substitute.

- When making vegetable soup, or beef, chicken, or tomato bouillon, add lemon juice and float thin lemon slices on top.
- When preparing broths or soups, add grated lemon peel and chopped parsley or chives in yogurt for garnish.
- In preparing salads, add fresh-squeezed lemon juice to shredded carrot-raisin salad.
- Embellish fruit salad with blended lemon juice and sugar.

- For meats, add thin slices of unpeeled lemon to meat-vegetable stews.
- For roasts, steaks, or chops, prepare a spicy hot sauce of blended lemon juice, dry mustard, and freshly ground black pepper.
- For baking or broiling poultry, brush with a blend of oil, lemon juice, and poultry seasoning; then dust with paprika.
- For frying poultry, dip pieces in lemon juice; then shake in a mixture of flour, marjoram, thyme, and instant minced onion.
- For baking whole fish, sprinkle inside and out with fresh lemon juice; then baste with lemon juice, chopped parsley, and unsalted butter or margarine.
- For broiling fish, brush with melted unsalted butter or margarine, lemon juice, and dill weed or tarragon.
- For carrots, corn, potatoes, and squash, serve lemon butter composed of blended softened unsalted butter or margarine with lemon juice, grated lemon peel, and chopped green onion.
- For green vegetables, add dried basil or marjoram to unsalted lemon butter.
- For desserts, blend grated orange or lemon peel with softened vanilla ice cream.

11

Herbs and Friends

Every herb is different from every other herb, each with special characteristics. For example, some of the more delicately flavored types should be put in sauces and soups only toward the end of cooking and left in just long enough to lose their volatile oils.

You can mix herbs together, but it's best not to use too many different kinds at the same time, or too much of any one kind. Moderation is the key to the use of herbs and the way to achieve maximum effectiveness with them.

In the list below I've tried to give a brief description of each herb and its flavor or fragrance, along with a list of its most common uses. Along with spices, herbs are most important in the war on salt as the premier seasoning agent.

The herbs appear in alphabetical order and not necessarily in the order of importance. I've made no attempt to compose a complete list; there are literally hundreds of marvelous herbs to use in flavoring food.

THE ANISES

There are many varieties of the anise plant, which provides not only leaves for garnishing and flavoring salads, but also seeds that can be ground up and powdered for use as a subtle flavoring. Anise has a strangely lingering licorice overtone, not so strong as licorice, but pleasant and penetrating.

The anise seed can be used to flavor any number of foods, from sponge cake to watermelon pickle. To release the full flavor of the seeds, crush them with a rolling pin.

The anise leaf can be used for garnishing and flavoring salads. The leaf is not so licorice-oriented as the seed.

THE BASILS

There are varieties of basil, called *l'herbe royal* by the French, which grow a sweet-flavored leaf with a fragrance suggesting lemon, anise, resin, and spice. Basil is a member of the mint family. It can be served in a bouquet of sprigs set in a small vase of water for individual flavoring.

Sweet basil, the most popular of the basils, can be used for a wide variety of purposes:

With Main Courses: beef, chicken, duck, lamb, lobster, pork, shrimp, turkey, veal, venison.

With Soups: lentil soup, minestrone, pea soup, tomato soup, vegetable soup.

With Salads: egg salad, potato salad, tomato aspic, tossed green salad.

With Vegetables: carrots, cauliflower, eggplant, peas, potatoes, spinach, squash.

And With: croutons, meatballs, pizzas, stuffings.

THE BAYS

The leaf of the bay tree family has a strong aromatic flavor. Bay leaf can be used fresh or dried. It should be used with discretion, only about one-third of a fresh leaf or one-sixth of a dried leaf in a quart of stew. If used in powdered form, a pinch will always suffice.

Bay leaf works well in the cooking of meats and vegetables, in the preparation of soups, stews, and gravies, and in the mixing of sauces and marinades.

NOTE: Bay leaf is a member of the laurel family, and is confined to the edible bay and *laurus nobilis.* Do not confuse it with the cherry laurel, *prunus laurocerasus*, which is a garden tree producing a poisonous leaf.

CARAWAY

The caraway plant, parsley-like in appearance, has small aromatic seeds that are similar to cumin in flavor. Caraway is a member of the carrot family. Caraway seeds should be used sparingly, as their flavor goes a long way.

Caraway can be used as a classic addition to asparagus, cabbage, cheese, marinades, rye bread, sauerkraut, stew, and turnips, and is the key flavor of kümmel.

Protracted heating makes caraway seed bitter; heat for only thirty minutes. To add flavor to vegetables or salads, crush caraway seeds first to release their flavor.

In addition, caraway can be used for a variety of purposes:

With Main Dishes: beef stew, duck, lamb stew, macaroni and cheese, tuna casserole.

With Soups: borscht, corn soup, pea soup, potato soup, vegetable soup.

With Salads: cucumber salad, potato salad.

With Vegetables: carrots, potatoes, squash.

And With: dips and spreads.

CELERY SEEDS

This completely misnamed herb does not come from the celery plant, nor is it a seed. It comes from a plant in the parsley family and is the brown seed-like fruit of the plant. It is called celery seed because it tastes like celery and looks like a seed.

Its uses include:

With Main Dishes: broiled fish, chicken, Cornish hen, duck, goose, macaroni and cheese, meat loaf, omelets, oyster stew, pot roast, stews, tuna casseroles, turkey.

With Soups: asparagus soup, lentil soup, pea soup, tomato soup, vegetable soup.

With Salads: cole slaw, dressing for fruit salad, egg salad, macaroni salad, potato salad, stuffed eggs.

With Vegetables: asparagus, broccoli, corn, okra, onions, potatoes, tomatoes.

And With: biscuits, dips, dumplings, pickles, rolls, stuffings, tomato sauce.

CHERVIL

Chervil is a member of the parsley family, only more delicate and fernlike. The flavor of the leaf resembles anise. Chervil must be grown and used fresh. When dried it has practically no flavor.

Chervil can be used to give special flavor to breads, cabbage dishes, cheeses, and some meat dishes, and to act as a garnish for chicken, omelets, green salad, spinach, and veal. It is the principal herb used in the making of vinaigrette sauce and is used, along with tarragon, in béarnaise sauce.

C H I V E S

Chives resemble small green onions. Both the taste and the smell are similar. They have a much more subtle and less penetrating taste than onions and can be used for dishes that need a slight touch of the flavor, not a surfeit.

Chives are used in white cheeses, in green sauces, and with eggs. They are best when cut and added to hot and cold food just before serving.

NOTE: Do not put chives in food that will be stored even as long as overnight. The flavor intensifies and becomes unpleasant.

Uses include:

With Main Dishes: fish, omelets, spaghetti.

With Soups: generally with all flavors.

With Salads: potato salad and most others.

With Vegetables: generally with all vegetables.

C O R I A N D E R

Coriander can be used both in leaf form and in seed form. The dried leaf has a subtle sage flavor. The dried seed develops a flavor resembling orange, anise, and cumin.

Fresh coriander is known differently in various countries: as *cilantro* in the Caribbean, *kothamille* in Mexico, and *dhuma* in India; it is translated as parsley in China. Float the fresh leaf (no stems) in pea or chicken soup, and in stews. Put the leaf on top of a roast, or use it in a bouillon for clams.

The whole seed can be used in marinades, pickles, punch, or soups.

The crushed seed has a variety of uses:

With Main Dishes: chicken, fish, hamburgers, meat pies, pork.

With Desserts: apple dishes, cakes, cookies, fruit pies, steamed puddings.

And With: biscuits, cornbread, Danish pastry, gingerbread, seasoned butter, stuffings.

CUMIN

Cumin, a member of the parsley family, has a classic, nutty flavor, very aromatic and even somewhat hot. The seed can be used either whole or ground up. It serves as the principal ingredient not only in curry but in chili powder as well.

It can be used whole or ground in a variety of foods:

With Main Dishes: dried bean dishes, fish, game, hamburgers, meat generally, meat loaf, Mexican-style dishes, pot roast, stews.

With Soups: lentil soup, pea soup, Middle Eastern soups.

With Salads: cabbage dishes, cucumbers, egg dishes, potato salad, salad dressings.

With Vegetables and Grains: corn, rice.

And With: tomato sauces.

DILLSEED AND DILLWEED

Dill has a distinct odor and flavor that is difficult to describe—pungent and slightly bitter, but memorable. A member of the carrot family, both stem and leaf can be used as dillweed; the seed is used as dillseed.

As dillweed (stem and leaf), dill can be used:

With Main Dishes: baked fish, broiled fish, chicken, sautéed shrimp, scrambled eggs.

With Salads: potato salad, salad dressings, stuffed eggs, tossed green salad, tuna salad.

With Vegetables: beets, carrots, cauliflower, potatoes, rice.

And With: bread, canapes, dips, and noodles.

Dillseed should be cleaned and dried with great care. Then it can be used:

With Main Dishes: fish, shellfish.

With Salads: cabbage, beets, salad dressings.

With Vegetables: cauliflower, green beans.

And With: dill pickles.

THE FENNELS

The seeds and leaves of the fennel plant both have a faint anise scent. As a plant, fennel is fragrant, beautiful, and graceful. It can be used as a salad arrangement as well as food. The leaf and seed also have an anise-like taste.

Fennel gives fatty fish a good flavor, and it works well in lentils, rice, and potatoes. The seed can be used to flavor apple pie. Fennel twigs burned to cook fish can add to its flavor. Use the leaf in sauces, but do not let them cook long enough to wilt, unless they have been blanched. The leaf does not retain flavor when dried.

In general, fennel can be used:

With Main Dishes: fish, oyster dishes, spiced shrimp.

With Salads: potato salad.

With Vegetables: artichokes, broccoli, brussels sprouts, cauliflower, potatoes.

With Desserts: apple cakes, baked apples.

And With: breads, sausage, spaghetti sauce, tomato sauce.

GARLIC

Garlic is a member of the lily family, brother to the onion, with a strong and distinct odor and flavor. It can be used as a bulb with its many cloves, or it can be used in powder or salt form. Garlic should be used sparingly, and to taste. It can be overpowering, even in scanty portions.

Some of its seasoning uses include:

With Main Dishes: baked fish, beef, broiled fish, game, lamb, pork, seafood dishes, variety meats, veal.

With Salads: green salads, salad dressings.

With Vegetables: eggplant, green beans, tomatoes.

And With: bread, pizza sauce, spaghetti sauce, tomato sauce.

THE MARJORAMS

There are several varieties of marjoram, one of which is the oregano plant, listed separately in this chapter. The marjoram plant itself is attractive, smooth, and green, with tiny green balls hanging from stems like ornaments on a Christmas tree. The leaf becomes the seasoning. It has a sweet, tangy taste.

Use it:

With Main Dishes: baked fish, beef, broiled fish, chicken dishes, game, lamb, meatballs, omelets, pork, scrambled eggs, variety meats.

With Soups: minestrone, tomato soup, vegetable soup.

With Salads: stuffed eggs, tossed green salad.

With Vegetables: artichoke, asparagus, beans, beets, broccoli, brussels sprouts, carrots, cauliflower, celery, mushrooms, onions, peas, spinach, summer squash, tomatoes, zucchini.

And With: cheese sauce, cornbread, dips, hollandaise sauce, stuffings, tomato juice, tomato sauce.

THE MINTS

There are a variety of mint plants. In addition to peppermint and spearmint, there are flavors like apple mint, orange mint, and pineapple mint. The mint is an aromatic herb, the leaf of which is used for flavoring.

It can be used principally:

With Main Dishes: lamb, meat dishes, veal.

With Salads: cole slaw.

With Vegetables: beans, beets, carrots, peas, potatoes, spinach, zucchini.

With Fruits: fruit cups, melons, oranges, pineapple.

And With: candies, cream cheese, in chocolate combinations, some desserts, jellies, juleps, sauces, teas.

THE MUSTARDS

The base mustard ingredient is a powder made of the mustard seed, the dry residue left after the oil is removed. It has a familiar hot, sharp flavor. You can purchase it in powdered form or in paste form. Commercial preparations contain a great deal of sodium, unless otherwise stated.

Mustard can be used widely to season all types of food:

With Main Dishes: beef, chicken, Cornish hen, duck, fish, game, goose, lamb, meatballs, omelets, pork, seafood, turkey, variety meats, veal.

With Soups: chicken soup, chowders, lentil soup, potato soup, tomato soup, vegetable soup.

With Salads: chicken salad, cole slaw, mayonnaise dressing, pickled eggs, potato salad.

With Vegetables: asparagus, cabbage, cauliflower, celery, corn, peas, spinach.

And With: cheese, cucumber pickles, dips, sandwich condiments, tomato sauce.

OREGANO

Oregano is a part of the marjoram family, with a strong but pleasantly bitter taste. Its flavor resembles marjoram but is stronger. It is available as a dried leaf or in crushed or ground forms.

Its use gives an Italian or Mexican flavor to cooking, in cheeses, eggs, meat dishes, and tomato sauces. Use it also:

With Main Dishes: baked fish, beef, broiled fish, chicken dishes, game, hamburgers, lamb, meatballs, meatloaf, omelets, pork, tuna casseroles, veal.

With Soups: chowders, lentil soup, minestrone, onion soup, tomato soup, vegetable soup.

With Salads: cottage cheese, Italian dressing, mayonnaise dressing, stuffed eggs.

With Vegetables: beans, carrots, eggplant, peas, potatoes, spinach, squash, tomatoes, turnips.

And With: croutons, dips, rolls, spaghetti sauce, tomato sauce.

THE PARSLEYS

The parsley family produces plants whose root, stem, and leaves can all be used to flavor food. Parsley can be used fresh or dried, and it garnishes as well as seasons. The plant can be used to tone down the scent of garlic and onion without destroying the flavor. There are about thirty-seven varieties of curly parsley alone. It is the best-known of all herbs.

It can be used:

With Main Dishes: baked fish, broiled fish, chicken dishes, hamburgers, meatloaf, omelets, pot roast, scrambled eggs, stews, veal dishes.

With Soups: as garnish for most soups.

With Salads: chicken salad, egg salad, herb dressing, Italian dressing, potato salad, stuffed eggs, tuna salad.

With Vegetables: asparagus, beets, carrots, cauliflower, eggplant, mushrooms, onions, peas, potatoes, rice.

And With: dips, rolls, stuffings.

RED AND GREEN PEPPERS

Cayenne, also called red pepper or chili pepper, is a powder made from the fruit of the capsicum plant. Other pepper herbs come from the same family. Capsicum varieties include red and green peppers, long and round peppers, and even yellow and chartreuse peppers.

The red, or chili, pepper has a hot, biting taste. Chili is the flavor that gives Mexican food its bite. It is too hot to be used except in very small, controlled amounts.

Use to flavor cheese dishes, meat dishes, and spicy sauces.

ROSEMARY

Rosemary is a sweet-flavored leaf of the mint family. It is extremely pungent and must be handled with caution, although the end result is a spicy sweetness.

Use it:

With Main Dishes: baked fish, beef, capon, chicken dishes, duck, lamb, partridge, pizza, poached fish, rabbit, stew, veal, venison.

With Soups: beef broth, chicken soup, minestrone, pea soup, tomato soup, vegetable soup.

With Vegetables: brussels sprouts, cabbage, carrots, cauliflower, green beans, lima beans, potatoes, tomatoes, turnips, zucchini.

And With: cornbread, fruit juice, herb dressing, spaghetti sauce, stuffing, tomato juice.

SAFFRON

Saffron has a slightly bitter taste, but its chief use is in coloring food yellow or orange. When dried, saffron lets off a strong aroma. It is made from the dried golden stigmas of a variety of crocus. It takes seventy-five thousand blossoms to produce one pound of saffron powder.

Use it in Spanish, French, and Italian dishes, especially those containing rice. For coloring, use sparingly. For flavoring, follow directions carefully. You can use it to flavor breads, cakes, some international dishes, rice, and soups generally.

SAGE

The leaf of the sage has a pungent, slightly bitter taste, and an aroma similar to that of thyme. It is one of the most widely used herbs in the United States. The leaf can be dried or ground up.

Use it to season meat dishes, sauces, soups and stuffings.

It fortifies vinegar marinades as well. Also use it:

With Main Dishes: beef, cheese casserole, chicken, duck, egg casserole, fish, goose, lamb, meatballs, meatloaf, omelets, pork, pot roast, stews, turkey, veal, venison.

With Soups: chicken soup, chowders, minestrone, tomato soup, vegetable soup.

With Vegetables: brussels sprouts, eggplant, lima beans, onions, peas, potatoes, summer squash, tomatoes.

And With: dumplings, gravies, herb dressings, stuffings.

THE SAVORIES

Savory comes in two main varieties, summer savory and winter savory. The leaf of summer savory is a much more delicately flavored herb than winter savory. Summer savory has a more subtle taste; it resembles thyme. Winter savory is a rather resinous perennial, the leaves of which can be used in stews, stuffings, and meat loaves.

Use summer savory with green beans and green bean salad. Use it in horseradish sauce and lentil soup. Use it also in deviled eggs. It can also be used with fat fish, in French dressings, with potatoes, roast pork, and with tomatoes.

Use winter savory with chicken or turkey dishes, meat pies, stews, with stuffings, herb waffles, broccoli, brussels sprouts, green beans, lima beans, tomato soup, and vegetable soup.

SESAME SEEDS

The seed of the sesame plant is used as a favorite topping for breads, cookies, and vegetables. Sesame has a nutty flavor that is brought out when the seeds are lightly toasted and stirred frequently. Crushed sesame seeds turn into an oily paste that is called tahina. Chick-peas (garbanzo beans) can be mixed with crushed sesame and other spices to make hummus with tahina. The oil from the sesame seed is a much desired salad oil.

Uses for the sesame seed include:

With Main Dishes: dumplings, fried chicken, scrambled eggs, steaks, veal dishes.

With Salads: cottage cheese, fruit salad, salad dressing, tomatoes, tossed green salad.

With Vegetables: asparagus, mushrooms, vegetable casseroles.

And With: bread, biscuits, cakes, cookies, pastry, stuffings, waffles.

TARRAGON

The aromatic leaf of tarragon has a flavor slightly reminiscent of licorice. It is called *estragon* by the French. The dried leaf loses much of the original flavor of the fresh leaf.

Because of its pungency, tarragon cannot be used with freshly cooked soups, but can be used with almost anything else. It is the principal herb used in the making of béarnaise sauce.

Try it:

With Main Dishes: chicken, egg dishes, fish, game, shellfish, sweetbreads, turkey.

With Salads: salad dressing, tossed green salads.

With Vegetables: asparagus, beans, brussels sprouts, eggplant, tomatoes, mushrooms, yellow turnips.

And With: béarnaise sauce, eggs, marinades, mustard sauce, pickles, tartar sauce.

THE THYMES

Many varieties of thyme exist. All are members of the mint family. Thyme has a strong, distinctive flavor, warm and aromatic.

Use thyme:

With Main Dishes: baked fish, beef, broiled fish, cheese dishes, chicken, duck, dumplings, fruit dishes, game, goose, lamb, liver, meatballs, pizza, pork, variety meats, veal.

With Soups: chicken soup, chowders, gumbos, minestrone, tomato soup, vegetable soup.

With Vegetables: asparagus, beans, beets, broccoli, carrots, eggplant, green beans, mushrooms, onions, potatoes, spinach, tomatoes, white turnips, yellow turnips, zucchini.

And With: gravies, spaghetti sauce, stuffings, tomato juice.

12

Spices and Friends

Like herbs, every spice is different from every other spice, each having special characteristics. Because spices provide strong seasoning for foods, most of them should be used sparingly.

In the list below I've tried to give a brief description of the spice and its flavor or fragrance, along with a list of foods with which it is most commonly and most effectively used.

ALLSPICE

Allspice is the pea-sized fruit of a West Indian tree, known for its sharp, many-faceted flavor. Within its small reddish brown berry is a mixture of flavors like cinnamon, clove, nutmeg, and juniper berry. From that fact comes the name allspice. The French call it *quatre épices*—four spices, a more accurate name. The allspice berry is dried and ground into a powder for use.

Use it whole in fish dishes, gravies and with meats. Use

135

it ground in or on cakes, cookies, fruit, fruit pies, roasts, preserves, puddings, relishes, tomato sauce, and steak. In general, you can use allspice from soup to nuts, alone or in combination with other spices.

THE CARDAMOMS

The cardamom plant is a member of the ginger family. Its seed, dried and ground up, has a sweet and pungent flavor. It should be powdered just before use, otherwise it loses its aromatic flavor. The seed has a versatile affinity that provides a broad range of uses from the daintiest dessert to the flavor for sausage and curry.

Cardamom can be used in place of cinnamon and cloves, alone, or in combination. It tastes great in coffee. Its use gives Scandinavian and Indian flavors to cooking. It is used in curry, but can be used in pastries as well.

Some of its uses include:

With Main Dishes: baked beans, poached fish, pork roast, pot roast.

With Soups: green pea soup.

With Fruits: fruit salads, fruit salad dressings.

With Vegetables and Grains: rice, squash, sweet potatoes.

With Desserts: cakes, cookies, custard, Danish pastry, gingerbread.

And With: French toast.

THE CINNAMONS

The true cinnamon, *cinnamomum zeylanicum*, is the bark of a tree that grows in Sri Lanka and along the Malabar

Coast. Rolled in a tight quill or stick, or in powdered form, it is a mild spice with an aromatic, sweet, pungent taste.

However, most commercial cinnamon is cassia, *cinnamomum cassia*, a similar bark formed like a short scroll. The taste is slightly bitter compared to the warm, sweet, aromatic true cinnamon.

It can be used in stick form in cider, coffee, fruit compotes, hot chocolate, mulled wine, and pickles. In ground form, it can be used on cookie tops or on toast; it can also be incorporated into desserts and baked items like rolls, spice cake, pudding, and pumpkin pie.

NOTE: Cinnamon sugar is a perfect blend of ground cinnamon and sugar used to make cinnamon toast. It can also be sprinkled over baked apples, coffee cakes, cookies, cupcakes, French toast, pancakes, stewed fruit, and waffles.

Among its other uses are:

With Main Dishes: Eastern meat dishes of beef, chicken, and pork.

With Fruits: apples, apricots, blueberries, cherries, compotes, cranberries, figs, grapefruit, peaches, pears, pineapple, plums, prunes, rhubarb.

With Vegetables: sweet potatoes and yellow squash.

CHILI POWDER

Chili powder is a blend of several herbs and spices, including cumin, garlic, and oregano, with cloves and allspice sometimes added. It is the essential ingredient in certain Mexican dishes.

It can be used generally in sauces, stews, and in meat dishes.

CLOVES

The dried brown bud of the evergreen clove tree has a warm, spicy, pungent taste when dried either whole or ground up. Because its flavor is so strong, the heads of the cloves should be removed to make the seasoning milder. Be sure to take out any whole cloves used in cooking prior to serving. Oil of clove can be purchased for use in light-colored foods; it has a strong pungency.

Cloves can be used:

With Main Dishes: Eastern dishes, eggs, ham, tongue, various meats.

With Fruits: apples, apricots, blueberries, cherries, cranberries, lemon, lime, peaches, pears, plums, prunes, rhubarb.

With Vegetables: beets, cabbage, carrots, onion, yellow squash.

With Mixes: chutney, curry, ketchup, marinades, marmalades, pickled dishes, sauces, special syrups, stewed fruit.

And With: desserts, mulled wines, teas.

CURRY

Curry powder is actually a blend of about sixteen separate spice flavors, including cumin and other seeds, several varieties of cayenne, coriander, ginger, red pepper, turmeric, and sometimes allspice and cinnamon. Curry powder is really best when it is freshly ground and incorporated into a paste with onion, garlic, and fruits and vegetables like apples and carrots or tamarind and pomegranate.

Curry powder should be specially blended for each kind of dish: sour for marinated meats; dry for coating meat;

other mixtures in between for chicken or mutton, beans, fish, rice and vegetables. Curry ranges from extremely hot to mild. As a balance to curry powder, drink beer or a tart limeade when eating it.

Its uses include:

With Main Dishes: beef, chicken, Indian-style cooking, lamb, lobster, meatballs, oysters, pork, rice-egg casseroles, scrambled eggs, seafood dishes, shrimp, stews, turkey.

With Soups: curry soup and soups generally.

With Salads: curried egg, French dressing, mayonnaise, seafood salad, stuffed egg, sour cream dressing.

With Vegetables: beans, broccoli, brussels sprouts, cabbage, corn, creamed vegetables, onions, potatoes, summer squash.

And With: curry sauce, dips, rolls.

GINGER

Ginger is the root of a plant grown in the Orient and Central America. It is available preserved (green) or dried and cured. It comes in slivers, or ground up. Ground ginger, after being dried and cured, can be obtained in two forms. When the skin is left on the root, it is called black ginger. When the skin is removed, it is called white ginger. Ginger comes candied also, and can in this form be washed of its sugar and substituted for fresh ginger.

Ginger can be used:

With Main Dishes: beef, baked fish, chicken casserole, duck, Far Eastern meat dishes, roast chicken, roast pork, turkey, veal, venison.

With Soups: chicken soup, chowders.

With Fruits: apples, cherries, cranberries, figs, fruit salads, grapefruit, peaches, pears, pineapple, rhubarb.

With Vegetables: carrots, onions, peas, squash, sweet potatoes.

With Desserts: cakes, cookies, custard, dessert sauces, gingerbread, pudding.

And With: baked goods, cooked fruits, French toast, gravies, pastry, sauces, toast.

MACE

Mace comes from the nutmeg tree and appears as a fleshy orange-red skin of the fruit of this evergreen tree. Mace has a softer flavor than nutmeg, warm and spicy and a little more pungent. It is available in powdered form. It can be used in baking, in sauces, in pumpkin dishes, and in some meat and fish dishes.
Uses include:

With Main Dishes: lamb, meatballs.

With Soups: chicken soup, chowder.

With Vegetables: carrots, potatoes, spinach, sweet potatoes.

With Fruits: apples, peaches, pineapple.

With Desserts: cakes, cookies, custard, dessert sauce, eggnog, pudding, stewed fruits.

And With: coffee cake, doughnuts, gravies.

NUTMEG

Nutmeg comes from the nutmeg tree, appearing as the hard inner kernel of the tree's fruit. The kernel can be used whole or ground up. It has a spicy flavor, stronger than that of its close relative, mace. For full flavor, grind nutmeg fresh in a nutmeg grinder, which works like a pepper mill.

Nutmeg can be used in baking and to season food much in the manner of mace. Its uses include:

With Main Dishes: most meat dishes.

With Vegetables: asparagus, beans, beets, broccoli, brussels sprouts, cabbage, carrots, cauliflower, onions, peas, spinach, summer squash.

With Fruits: apples, blueberries, cherries, cranberries, lemon, lime, pineapple, rhubarb.

And With: dessert sauces and pudding.

PAPRIKA

Paprika, a mixture of various ground peppers, comes mainly from plants that resemble tomatoes or bell peppers. It can be used both to decorate food and to flavor it. It gives a Hungarian flavor to cooking, used on roasts, poultry, eggs, in soups, and with corn, cauliflower, onions, and potatoes.

NOTE: Paprika is sometimes categorized as an herb, but because it is a mixture of various types of red peppers, it should be considered a spice.

Its uses include:

With Main Dishes: broiled fish, cheese dishes, fried chicken, macaroni, tuna, veal.

With Soups: with soups generally.

With Salads: French dressings, mayonnaise, potato salad, salad dressings of various types.

With Vegetables: asparagus, carrots, cauliflower, creamed vegetables, new potatoes, onions.

And With: creole sauce, eggs, garnishes.

BLACK AND WHITE PEPPERS

Both black and white pepper come from the berry of the *piper nigrum* (black pepper). Next to salt, pepper is probably one of the most commonly used of all condiments. When the pepper berry is dried and used in its whole form, it turns black and is called black pepper. In its whole form this dried berry is called a peppercorn. When the black peppercorn is ground up, ground black pepper results.

When the outer covering of the peppercorn is removed from the seed and the seed is ground up separately, white pepper results. White pepper is not nearly so strong as black pepper. It is also much more aromatic than black pepper. Black and white pepper can be used interchangeably.

Black pepper can be used in almost any food except sweets. Its flavor is much more palatable if it is freshly ground in a pepper mill. In addition to being a seasoning, pepper can also help preserve food flavors without masking them the way other spices do.

White pepper is used to flavor sausages and canned meats. Its flavor holds up much better than black pepper. White pepper is used in all light-colored foods and sauces so that it cannot be seen.

NOTE: The use of the word *pepper* in a recipe usually refers to black pepper. Use black pepper unless the recipe calls specifically for white pepper.

Some uses of black pepper include:

With Main Dishes: fish, meats, poultry.

With Soups: all soups generally.

With Vegetables: beans, cabbage, celery, eggplant, onions, peas, potatoes, spinach, tomatoes, zucchini.

And With: sauces generally.

P O P P Y   S E E D

The poppy seed comes from *papaver phoeas,* a poppy plant that is different from the opium poppy and the California golden poppy. The edible poppy seed comes from a plant that is slate blue. The seed is best when roasted or steamed and crushed before its use in cooking. Then the full flavor is released. It can be crushed in a small handmill.

It is usually used in baking. As a special garnish, it can be used on noodles.

Other uses include:

With Main Dishes: chicken casserole, chicken livers, macaroni and cheese, noodles, omelets, scrambled eggs, tuna casserole.

With Fruits: fruit compotes, mixed fruit salads.

With Vegetables and Grains: asparagus, carrots, potatoes, rice, squash, sweet potatoes, turnips.

With Desserts: cakes, cookies, dumpling, fillings.

And With: bread, cottage cheese, dips, French toast, garnish, spreads, stuffings, stuffing for pork chops.

VANILLA BEAN AND EXTRACT

The pod of the vanilla plant provides the material which, when fermented and cured for six months, becomes the vanilla bean. From this bean an extract is prepared by macerating the beans in an alcohol solution.

Vanilla should be added to food only when it is cooling, in order to obtain maximum flavor. The extract is used in the preparation of a variety of confections, beverages, and food dishes.

NOTE: Do not expect true vanilla flavor when you purchase synthetic vanillas; furthermore their flavor can ruin any dish that is frozen. Nonalcoholic liqueur seasonings also give a synthetic flavor rather than the true vanilla flavor.

Don't Use Salt—Use Herbs and Spices

(In addition to herbs and spices, other accompaniments are suggested for some of the following dishes.)

With Beef: bay leaf, dry mustard powder, fresh mushrooms, green pepper, marjoram, nutmeg, onion, pepper, sage, or thyme

With Chicken: fresh mushrooms, green pepper, lemon juice, marjoram, paprika, parsley, poultry seasoning, sage, or thyme

With Fish: bay leaf, curry powder, dry mustard powder, fresh mushrooms, green pepper, lemon juice, marjoram, or paprika

With Lamb: curry powder, garlic, mint, mint jelly, pineapple, or rosemary

With Peas: fresh mushrooms, green pepper, mint, onions, or parsley

With Pork: apple, applesauce, garlic, onion, or sage

With Potatoes: green pepper, onions, paprika, or parsley

With Rice: chives, green pepper, onion, pimiento, or saffron

With Veal: apricot, bay leaf, curry powder, ginger, marjoram, or oregano

NOTE: If you use fresh herbs in place of dried, you need two to three times as much. If you want to flavor with wines, use table wines; cooking wines usually contain added salt.

13

Watching Weight and Sodium Intake

One of the reasons Walter Kempner's rice diet was so successful in battling hypertension was its ability to keep the patient's weight down. Obesity has always been an enemy to the person with high blood pressure.

No low-sodium diet is in itself a surefire way to cut down weight. However, by limiting the amount of sodium in the system, the diet does cut down on the body's propensity to hold moisture and thus add to the body weight.

Certain patients on low-sodium crash diets (under the supervision of a doctor) may find that the limitation of salt intake automatically makes them lose poundage. However, after a few days, the weight will once again stabilize, but at a lower figure.

Nevertheless, a low-sodium diet does not automatically make the patient shed weight. To get rid of excess fat you have to put yourself on a regimen that cuts down the caloric intake too.

However, the very method of limiting sodium intake may help you take on a rigid dietary regimen. By counting milligrams of sodium you become accustomed to watching what goes into your stomach. This habit of watching your intake helps you watch your weight too.

Tips on Cutting Down Weight

Generally speaking, there are a number of tips you should know about weight watching. They are in their way as simple and as valuable as the tips on limiting sodium intake that I told you about in Chapter Five. Actually, some of the tips you learned there can be extended to help you control your cholesterol and carbohydrate intake. Some of the foods to concentrate on become "magic" nutrients that contain little sodium and also few calories.

For example, one of the special points I've already cautioned you about is the avoidance of commercial salad dressings because of their high sodium content. These concoctions also include ingredients that cause you to put on weight. But that's only one danger food. There are others.

Let's take a look at a list of commonsense tips on avoiding weight gain that are similar to tips on avoiding a high-sodium intake:

- Season food with herbs and spices rather than salt.
- If you can, always eat fresh food rather than canned or frozen.
- Eat fish and vegetables cooked with little salt, butter, margarine, or oil.
- Eat as many fresh fruits and vegetables as you can; avoid canned or frozen kinds if possible.

- Avoid eating the skin of any poultry item; it's helpful to remove the skin before cooking.
- Drink coffee or tea without sugar, cream, or whole milk.
- Avoid eating commercial salad dressings.
- Don't indulge yourself in pickles or other condiments of that kind.

As you can see, about half the basic tips for keeping slim are similar to tips on avoiding sodium. But there are several more that I'll touch on shortly. Meanwhile, I'd like to mention one of the key truths in keeping your weight down. It is, put quite simply, to consume food and drink *in moderation.* If you don't overindulge, the chances are that you won't be fat.

The word *overindulge* can be subject to misinterpretation. America is a country of abundance—in produce as well as in products. As a natural habit, we Americans eat a great deal more than the people of almost any other country on earth. The food is there, it's good, and so we eat it.

Besides, there's a certain amount of natural pride in having plenty. The person who has plenty to eat can be considered successful and blessed. A certain amount of prosperity shows through in a plump, well-fed exterior.

More Tips on Cutting Down Weight

In addition to practicing moderation in eating, here are a number of other helpful tips to observe in order to keep your weight down:

- Eat only as much as you need to fill you. Do *not* deliberately overeat.

- Be sure to eat slowly. Eating rapidly tends to lead to overeating.
- Make it a habit to avoid foods that have a lot of fat in them.
- If you do have fish, meat, or poultry with fat, trim it all away before you cook or eat.
- Bake, broil, or roast all foods, allowing excess fat to drip away.
- Eat low-fat milk and cheese.
- Never eat between meals. You'll always stimulate yourself to eating more than you should and tend to break down your strict regimen.
- Never skip a meal. The regularity of your meals and the pattern of eating will keep your intake within bounds.
- Substitute diet margarine for butter.

These general tips will help you to maintain a better and more moderate diet.

What Foods to Concentrate On

There are a number of good foods you should eat in order to keep your weight under control. Note that they are foods that do not have high-sodium content. If you follow these simple rules, and keep note of your sodium intake as well, you'll keep your weight within the proper limits and hold down your sodium consumption too.

MEAT, POULTRY, FISH

Eat two servings of meat, which is a high-protein food (or substitute high-protein vegetables such as soybeans or tofu), every day. In place of lean meat, eat poultry or fish. Lean meat includes all types—beef, fresh ham, lamb, rabbit, veal, and venison. Poultry includes turkey and chicken; other types of fowl have too much fat. All kinds of fish, including the shellfish low in cholesterol—clams, crabs, and scallops—are good.

NOTE: Do not use salt or rich sauces on these foods. Prepare them with herbs and spices.

VEGETABLES

Eat vegetables or salads daily. At least three or four times a week eat many vegetables which are high in vitamin A, B complex, C, and potassium. These include all regular vegetables and especially: broccoli, carrots, collards, kale, pumpkin, spinach, sweet potatoes, turnip greens, watercress, winter squash, and zucchini. Prepare them without the use of salt; if you use canned or frozen vegetables, make sure they are low-sodium preparations.

SOUPS

Eat only fresh soups, avoiding creamed soups, which contain fat. Stick to clear consommé, chicken broth, vegetable soup, and fish chowders, so long as they are fresh and contain no seasoning or sodium. To remove fat, chill soups. This will cause the fat to rise to the top, where it can then be skimmed off and discarded. Reheat and serve.

FRUITS

Eat fresh fruits daily; they contain high quantities of vitamin C. Include bananas, cantaloupes, grapefruit, mangoes, oranges, papayas, strawberries, tangerines, and the usual fruits in season. Many of these foods also contain potassium which is good food for hypertensive dieting.

EGGS

Eat up to three eggs a week—scrambled, poached, soft or hard boiled, sunny-side up—any way you like. If cholesterol is an issue for you, use an egg substitute, but, remember, cholesterol is only in the yolk. An omelet should not contain salt or any high-sodium ingredients. Don't fry an egg in butter; use a nonstick skillet.

MILK

Use low-sodium milk if possible. Buttermilk is low in fat, but high in sodium, with from 100 to over 300 milligrams per cup. Evaporated milk contains almost as much sodium as buttermilk. Look out for yogurt; a cup contains 100 to 230 milligrams of sodium. In spite of the sodium content, it is important to drink at least two cups of milk each day, or the equivalent in dairy products (one ounce of cheese, one cup of cottage cheese, one cup of homemade yogurt).

BREAD

Eat only about three slices of bread a day, or one roll and two slices of bread. Be sure to use only low-sodium bread, which contains only a trace of sodium. An ordinary slice of white or wheat bread will average 135 to 160 milligrams of sodium. You may make your own low-sodium breads.

OILS

Consume one or two teaspoons of liquid vegetable oil every day in salads or in cooking if possible. Use corn, cottonseed, safflower, soybean, or sunflower oil. Use margarine made from liquid vegetable oil and make sure that the first ingredient on the label states "liquid."

SALADS

Eat garden fresh salad greens like bibb, chicory, escarole, iceberg lettuce, romaine, watercress, and combine with cabbage, carrots, celery, endives, onions, radishes, scallions and tomatoes. Eat as much as you like, using lemon and herb or oil and vinegar dressings.

ALCOHOLIC BEVERAGES

Avoid sweetened cocktails like whiskey sours and old-fashioneds. Avoid mixers like colas and soft drinks. Select dry wines and avoid dessert wines. Don't use cordials or liqueurs; they are high in sugar. Use light beer. But remember, even regular beer is low in sodium. Rye, scotch, vodka, gin, or Canadian whiskey are okay; bourbon and Irish whiskey are too sweet. However, limit yourself to one daily glass of wine, jigger of hard liquor, or bottle or can of beer.

If you stick to the above suggestions, you will find yourself cutting down on your sodium intake *and* your caloric intake. Soon enough your sodium counting will begin to take effect and become a habit.

Low-Sodium, Low-Calorie Daily Menu

A typical daily menu to provide for low-sodium intake and low-caloric intake might include the following foods. (Refer to sodium intake list at the end of Chapter Six for amounts of each food.)

BREAKFAST

Fresh fruit juice.

Eggs, low-sodium peanut butter, low-sodium cheese, or rice.

Low-sodium, low-fat milk.

One slice of low-sodium wheat or white bread with margarine.

Coffee, tea, or herb tea.

COFFEE BREAK

Fruit, ½ cup low-fat cottage cheese, or graham crackers with low-sodium peanut butter and raisins.
Coffee, tea, herb tea.

LUNCH

Banana or any fruit you want.
Tossed green salad with noncommercial dressing containing little sodium.
Any fresh vegetable except potatoes.
COLD DISH: sandwich of lean meat, egg, low-sodium peanut butter, fish, chicken, or turkey, with fresh non-creamed soup.
or
HOT DISH: lean meat, chicken, fish, or egg, with fresh non-creamed soup, with one slice of low-sodium bread.
*Zingy Vegetable Dip, *Low-Sodium Munchies, sherbet, or sponge cake.
Coffee, tea, herb tea, or low-fat milk.

AFTERNOON COFFEE BREAK

Fruit, unsalted nuts, sliced banana with low-sodium peanut butter topping.
Coffee, tea, herb tea.

BEFORE-DINNER DRINK

Cocktail, hard liquor, beer, or wine.

*See recipes in Chapter Fifteen.

DINNER

Fresh fruit cocktail or seafood cocktail. (Note that shrimp contains 140 milligrams of sodium per serving; seafood cocktail sauce contains about 750 per serving.)

Any fresh noncreamed soup.

Any tossed green salad with low-sodium dressing.

Any freshly cooked vegetable (without salt).

Hot dish of lean meat, poultry, or fish, cooked without salt.

One slice of low-sodium wheat or white bread with unsalted margarine.

Angel food cake or sherbet or fresh melon and blueberries.

Coffee, tea, or herb tea.

14

Dining Out
the Salt–Free
Way

Getting my sodium intake under control in my own home
was enough of a problem at first. When I had finally mas-
tered the technique of planning for, shopping for, and preparing the food itself, I could say without fear of contradiction
that I had cut down my sodium intake to within my target
area.

However, when it came to dining out, I was very wary of
ever hoping to keep within my specified limits. Had I been
on a rigid sodium-controlled diet—1,000, 500, or 250 milligrams per day—I would have had to handle dining out
in a different manner.

I learned several basic rules almost immediately. And by
learning them, and later on innovating other procedures
as I went along, I was able to control my sodium intake a
great deal better than I had anticipated.

The main consideration was first to discover which dishes
prepared by someone else would be acceptable on a low-

sodium diet and which would not. The obvious procedure was to stick to dishes with foods that had a low natural sodium content and avoid dishes with a high natural sodium content.

It took some time to learn, but in the end I was able to make good guesses as to the general amount of sodium in the prepared dish set before me.

Dining out for me broke down into three different types of activity: lunch during working hours; dining out in a restaurant; and dining out at a friend's home.

To Brown Bag or Not to Brown Bag

Although taking a lunch along from home each morning was at one time looked down upon as the mark of the day laborer or the sweatshop worker, brown bagging recently invaded the corporate structure. In fact, the symbol of the quick lunch at the desk soon tended to create an image of the dedicated, upwardly mobile white-collar junior executive. It became popular to bring lunch from home, if not in a lunch box, then in a plain unmarked paper bag.

Here then was the natural outlet for any person interested in cutting down on sodium intake. A glance at the daily regimens in this book will show that a careless lunch can dramatically build up sodium intake. There are numerous ways in which you can actually cut down on excess sodium and guarantee to stay within reasonable limits.

The most efficient menu for a lunch at the desk is based on the familiar sandwich. Here are a few basic rules for creating low-sodium sandwiches:

• Prepare all sandwiches with only low-sodium bread. You can buy low-sodium bread at a regular supermarket in the freezer section, or you can bake your own. Keep it in your own freezer at home.

NOTE: There is a difference between salt-free bread and low-sodium bread. True low-sodium bread is made with low-sodium milk powder, or is a water-based product.

- Be sure to keep your sandwich fresh by storing it in an insulated bag. If you make it the night before for a quick getaway in the morning, freeze it flat and well-wrapped.

NOTE: Never freeze a sandwich containing a filling prepared with low-sodium mayonnaise, lettuce, or egg whites. These accompaniments are to be used the *same day only*; they rapidly deteriorate in texture if not used promptly. When you prepare them, refrigerate but do not freeze.

- Use a variety of fillings for your sandwiches so your lunch will not become monotonous. Here are a few choices that might prove satisfying:

  1. Try thin slices of roast beef. Beef has a natural sodium content, but not an excessive amount.
  2. Prepare a cold chicken or turkey sandwich, using cranberry sauce to flavor it.
  3. Low-sodium peanut butter combined with jelly, bananas, or alone is a good appetizer.
  4. A slice of pot roast spread with low-sodium piccalilli and lettuce makes a good low-sodium meal.
  5. Try second-day meat loaf in sandwich-size slices, with low-sodium mayonnaise.
  6. Try low-sodium water-packed tuna. Use low-sodium mayonnaise with it but in moderation because of the large number of calories.
  7. Try low-sodium water-packed salmon, flaked and mixed with low-sodium dressing.

8. If you want different flavors in your sandwiches, try some herbal shakers.

* In addition to a sandwich, take along some fruit in your brown bag. Fruit is splendidly low in natural sodium content. An apple, a peach, a pear, an orange, a tangelo (when in season of course) will give an added fillip to dessert, since these fruits are low in both sodium and calories.
* Don't bother to take along thermos bottles of hot coffee or tea to the office. Most office buildings have hot drink dispensers or even coffee shops. Lunch counters will usually prepare take-out beverages for you. Remember that your sodium problem does not lie in the area of coffee, tea, or other hot drinks.
* Slip your brown bag lunch into your attaché case, handbag, or briefcase. It does not have to be an unsightly appendage as you stroll into the office.

Brown bagging does not mean that you have to eat every day in the office at your desk. You can always vary your routine by dropping in at the neighboring lunch counter or the company cafeteria. Just be sure that the foods you select contain no excess sodium. A little practice and patience will teach you how to avoid it.

If you do decide to try a lunch counter near the office, pay attention to the tips in the following section.

Restaurant Dining
the Low-Sodium Way

Dining out is really not the ordeal it might be for the person anxious to maintain a low-sodium profile. There are several basic facts you must remember. Once you have them in mind, you can then determine what to select without any complicated juggling of foodstuffs.

First, let's analyze restaurant cooking for a moment. Most chefs in large eating places use a great deal of salt to cook vegetables. Salt, as you know, contains 40 percent sodium. It is then most important to avoid ordering vegetables, or to avoid eating them if served, in the average restaurant.

What makes vegetables even higher in sodium is that chefs tend to use not only salt in preparing vegetables, but baking soda as well. This unseen villain is a much-loved cooking aid because it keeps that fresh green color in the cooked vegetables.

Thus sodium may appear in two guises in most cooked vegetables—in salt and in baking soda—and therefore it is a good rule of thumb to stay away from cooked vegetables. Usually this is not a hardship for the average person.

The one vegetable you can order is potato. Baked potato is best. Do not salt it or use salted butter to flavor it. Small amounts of sour cream can be used, along with pepper and paprika.

Most gravy prepared in restaurants is heavy in salt. Stay away from it. You can substitute mint jelly, cranberry sauce, or applesauce; none of these condiments contain excess sodium. Gravy does.

When ordering a slice of any roasted meat in a restaurant, you can safely eat beef, lamb, poultry, fresh pork, or veal without fearing excess sodium. The one entrée to avoid is smoked ham or *any* kind of ham except fresh ham. Smoked ham contains a great deal of salt.

If you want to make sure you are getting that part of any meat that is least apt to contain natural sodium, select an inside cut. Remember that the chef will season the surface of any roast before putting it in to cook, usually using salt or some sodium condiment. The farther away your slice of meat lies from the surface the better.

Even with an inside cut, be sure to trim away the edges of the slice before you eat. Any sodium will quite probably be contained in the edges and not the center.

In poultry, dark meat contains a higher degree of natural sodium than white meat. Poultry skin also has a high degree of natural sodium. Stay away from dark meat and skin. For a minimum of sodium, choose the white meat only.

Avoid ordering restaurant fish that has been frozen. Such processed food has been liberally doused in a salt bath or brine before being frozen. Restaurants are sometimes diffident about admitting they use frozen products; be firm. If you have any doubts, order something else.

As for restaurant salads, they can be a real booby trap for the unwary. Their ingredients usually have some natural sodium content, although not an excessive amount. Some salad bars, however, serve greens sprinkled with preservatives containing sodium. The danger lies in the salad dressing. Do not use the chef's dressing. Use plain oil and vinegar, or even take along some herbal shakers. Usually anything else, like mayonnaise or cheese dressing, contains a high degree of sodium.

Dining at a Chinese restaurant can be a difficult adventure in eating out, especially if you are trying to reduce your sodium intake. Most Chinese food prepared for mass consumption is heavily flavored with monosodium glutamate. Soy sauce also contains a great deal of sodium. However, a good Chinese restaurant may cook to your order. Specify to the chef that the food be cooked with the addition of no salt or MSG.

When restaurant food comes to the table, do not use salt, but flavor it with pepper, sugar, and lemon juice.

To recapitulate, the main points in low-sodium restaurant dining are:

- Stay away from vegetables; they're cooked with salt.
- Avoid gravy on meat; it is heavy in salt.
- Don't order smoked ham.
- Specify an inside cut on any meat you are ordering.
- Order any chop or steak to be broiled without salt.
- Select white meat over dark meat in poultry.
- Order only fresh fish; avoid frozen.
- Avoid mayonnaise or salad dressings made with cheese.
- At a Chinese restaurant, have your food cooked to order.

Guess Who's Coming to Dinner

You should not really be too sensitive about your low-sodium regimen when you are asked to dine out with friends in their own home. Frankly, it is inconsiderate to specify a separate menu and find yourself eating something different from the other guests. It is an insult to your hosts.

Most heavy sodium saturation will occur in the hors d'oeuvres that are served before you sit down at the table. Snacks are heavily fortified with salt and other forms of sodium. The trick is to bypass most of these heavily flavored items. After all, you have no idea how much sodium is in any of them. Don't ask!

If you like, you can always take one small bite and then cut down on your sodium intake for several days afterward. It is possible to make an occasional compromise.

If the meal is served in buffet style, you should not have any trouble at all selecting the right foods and avoiding the wrong foods. Buffet dining allows you to control your intake a great deal more easily than courses served at the table.

However, if the meal is served at the table, you simply have to manage the amount of each helping, cutting back on those high in sodium. Vegetables, as pointed out already, are usually cooked in salted water. Simply go easy on them. Eat moderate portions of all meats, cutting back on the gravy. With poultry, eat the white meat without fear, but go easy on the dark.

For banquets that are given as dues-paying affairs, you should arrange for your own choice of food with the manager ahead of time. If the banquets or club affairs are free, then you cannot do much about them except go easy on the gravy, vegetables, and salad dressings.

NOTE: Most banquets and semiformal affairs serve liquor to your own specification. Remember that carbonated beverages of all kinds contain sodium. Remember that alcoholic beverages do not. Do not use carbonated water as a mixer, but substitute plain branch water or fruit juice.

15
Salt–Free Recipes

These low-sodium recipes are prepared without the use of salt or other condiments heavy in sodium. They make use of herbs, spices, and lemon juice for seasoning, and take advantage of low-sodium fruits and vegetables to cut down on natural sodium in foodstuffs.

Spinach and Mushroom Salad

1 pound fresh spinach
¼ pound fresh, snow-white, unblemished mushrooms
juice of ½ lemon
3 tablespoons wine vinegar
7 tablespoons vegetable oil
¼ teaspoon dry mustard
freshly ground pepper
2 hard-boiled eggs, coarsely chopped

166 The Joy of Living Salt-Free

Wash and dry spinach. Discard tough stems. Cut or tear leaves into bite-size pieces. Rinse and drain mushrooms. Cut into thin slices and sprinkle with lemon juice to prevent discoloration. Toss spinach and mushrooms together in salad bowl. Combine oil, vinegar, mustard, and pepper. Shake well or whisk. Pour over the salad and toss until leaves are coated with dressing. Lift onto individual plates and sprinkle with chopped egg.

Serves 4

Approximately 112 milligrams of sodium per serving

Spinach Surprise

1 pound fresh spinach, washed and trimmed
1 tablespoon horseradish

Place washed spinach leaves directly in covered pan (do not add water, as enough clings to the leaves to cook without sticking). Steam over low heat until cooked, about 5 to 10 minutes. Add horseradish and stir well. Serve immediately.

Serves 4 (¼ cup per serving)

Approximately 100 milligrams of sodium per cup

Chicken Salad on Lettuce

4 cups bite-size pieces cooked chicken breast
1 cup red apple chunks, unpeeled

½ cup walnuts, coarsely broken
¾ cup seedless grapes
½ cup cucumber, peeled, seeded, and diced
8 tablespoons low-sodium mayonnaise
1 head Boston Lettuce

Combine chicken, apple, nuts, grapes and cucumber. Mix
with just enough mayonnaise to moisten lightly. Serve on
lettuce leaves.

Serves 4

Approximately 111 milligrams of sodium per serving

Egg Salad Sandwich Filling

1 hard-boiled egg
1 tablespoon low-sodium mayonnaise
dash of curry powder

Mash ingredients thoroughly.

Serves 1

Approximately 61 milligrams of sodium per serving

Baked Macédoine

3 tablespoons vegetable shortening
1 tablespoon onion, chopped
2 tablespoons pimento, chopped

2 tablespoons flour
2 cups low-sodium canned tomatoes
1 cup frozen whole kernel corn
1½ cups cooked rice
1 hard-boiled egg, chopped
1 tablespoon parsley, chopped
⅛ teaspoon pepper
1 teaspoon Worcestershire sauce
½ cup low-sodium cheddar cheese, grated

Preheat oven to 400° F. Melt vegetable shortening, add onion and pimento, and cook 3 minutes. Add flour and mix well. Add tomatoes and stir until mixture thickens slightly. Add corn, rice, egg and seasonings. Put in baking dish, sprinkle cheese over the top, and bake for 20 minutes.

Serves 4

Approximately 56 milligrams of sodium per serving

Cucumber Salad

2 cucumbers
2 tablespoons low-sodium French dressing
2 sprigs fresh dill, minced

Chill, pare, and slice cucumbers. Combine with French dressing. Sprinkle with freshly minced dill.

Serves 4

Approximately 4 milligrams of sodium per serving

Cole Slaw

²/₃ cup raw cabbage, shredded
1 tablespoon salad oil
1½ tablespoons vinegar
1 tablespoon Zesty Shaker
pinch of sugar

Mix oil, vinegar, Zesty Shaker, and sugar, then pour over cabbage.

Serves 1 or 2

Approximately 20 milligrams of sodium per ²/₃ cup

Baked Flounder Fillets

1½ pounds flounder fillets
1½ cups milk
ground black pepper
3 tablespoons unsalted butter
3 tablespoons flour
¼ pound low-sodium Cheddar cheese, coarsely grated
3 tablespoons lemon juice
paprika

Preheat oven to 350° F. Roll each fillet (split lengthwise if 8 inches or longer) and place in a 10-inch × 6-inch × 2-inch baking dish. Pour one cup of the milk over the fish rolls and sprinkle with pepper. Place in oven and bake about 30 minutes, or until fillets flake easily when tested with fork but are still moist. When fish fillets are done, remove from oven. Turn oven to broil. Melt butter in the top of a double boiler. Spoon most of the milk from the baking dish into a large measuring cup and then pour in remaining milk. Stir flour into melted butter in double boiler and then stir milk in slowly. Cook sauce over boiling water, stirring until thickened. Add cheese and stir until melted. Add lemon juice last. Carefully pour sauce over baked fish fillets and sprinkle with paprika. Brown fish lightly under broiler.

Serves 4

Approximately 174 milligrams of sodium per serving

Broiled Fish Fillets with Vegetables

1½ pounds haddock fillets
2 tablespoons salad oil
2 teaspoons lemon juice
½ teaspoon dried marjoram
2 tablespoons white wine
black pepper
4 medium-size white potatoes, cooked and quartered
2 tomatoes, halved
2 tablespoons unsalted margarine, melted
paprika
low-sodium bread crumbs
¼ teaspoon dried thyme

Preheat broiler. Arrange fish fillets with skin sides down on lightly oiled broiler pan. In small saucepan mix oil, lemon juice, marjoram, wine, and dash of black pepper. Warm the mixture. Spoon half of it over the fish. Arrange the quartered potatoes and halved tomatoes on the broiler pan. Brush the potatoes with melted margarine and sprinkle with paprika. Brush tomato halves with oil and sprinkle with bread crumbs and thyme. Place broiler pan under heat. Baste fish fillets several times with the remaining liquid and broil until fish is easily flaked with fork but still moist. Broiling time: (for fillets 1/4-inch to 1-inch thick) 2 inches from heat, 6 to 10 minutes. Do not turn.

Serves 4

Approximately 120 milligrams of sodium per serving

Chicken Breasts in White Wine Sauce

4 chicken breasts, skinned and boned (6 ounces each)
2 cups white wine
1 can low-sodium cream of mushroom soup
freshly ground pepper
2 tablespoons low-sodium butter
paprika

Preheat oven to 350° F. Lay chicken breasts on sheet of foil large enough to wrap around chicken in roasting pan. Blend wine, soup, and pepper. Pour over chicken and dot with butter. Fold in foil, seal tightly, and place in roasting pan. Bake 35 to 40 minutes. Turn out onto heated deep platter, dust with paprika, and serve.

Serves 4

Approximately 95 milligrams of sodium per serving

Lamb Curry

1½ pounds boneless lamb shoulder cut into 2-inch cubes
¼ cup flour
3 tablespoons vegetable shortening
1 clove garlic, minced
1 cup onions, sliced
2 small apples, pared and sliced
½ to 1 teaspoon curry powder
2 tablespoons brown sugar
¼ cup raisins
1 lemon, sliced
2 tablespoons shredded coconut
½ cup walnuts, chopped
1 cup water

Roll meat in flour. Melt shortening in large skillet over moderate heat. Add garlic and onions and cook until tender. Add meat and cook 10 minutes, stirring frequently. Add apples and curry powder. Simmer 5 minutes, stirring occasionally. Stir in the remaining ingredients. Cover and simmer 1 hour. Serve lamb curry over hot rice.

Serves 4

Approximately 100 milligrams of sodium per serving

Saucy Baked Pork Chops

4 loin pork chops, ½-inch or more thick
paprika
½ cup hot water
1 medium onion, sliced

½ small green pepper, cut in strips
1 cup white rice, cooked
¼ teaspoon cumin
1 can low-sodium tomato sauce

Preheat oven to 350° F. Sprinkle paprika on both sides of chops. Brown them in a lightly greased skillet. Place chops in baking dish. Add hot water, onion slices and pepper strips. Bake covered for 30 minutes. Remove from oven. Place mound of rice on each chop. Add cumin to tomato sauce and pour sauce over rice. Cover and return to oven to bake for 30 minutes more, or until done.

Serves 4

Approximately 85 milligrams of sodium per serving

Shish Kebab

¼ cup dry red wine
¼ cup olive oil
2 tablespoons onion, grated
1 teaspoon coriander seeds, crushed
1 teaspoon ground ginger
1 teaspoon turmeric
1 clove garlic, minced
2 pounds boneless lamb, cut into 1½-inch cubes
6 small onions, parboiled 5 minutes
6 medium mushroom caps
6 cherry tomatoes
6 squares green pepper
6 small potatoes, parboiled and quartered
2 tablespoons melted unsalted butter

Mix together the wine, oil, grated onion, crushed coriander seeds, ginger, turmeric, and garlic. Marinate the meat cubes in the mixture for 2 hours in refrigerator. Use six skewers and alternately place meat, onions, tomatoes, mushroom caps, green peppers, and potatoes on them, starting and ending with meat. Place in oven broiler, turning the skewers frequently and basting with butter. Broil 8 to 10 minutes, or to desired degree of doneness.

Serves 6

Approximately 116 milligrams of sodium per serving

Western Tamale Pie

1 cup yellow corn meal
2¼ cups boiling water
2 tablespoons unsalted margarine

2 tablespoons olive oil
1 large onion, diced
½ cup green pepper, diced
1 clove garlic, minced
1 pound ground chuck, browned
2½ cups canned low-sodium tomatoes
1 cup frozen or fresh corn
1 tablespoon chili powder
¼ teaspoon allspice
¼ teaspoon black pepper
4 ripe olives, sliced
¼ pound low-sodium Cheddar cheese, grated

In top of double boiler stir corn meal into boiling water. Stir constantly until thickened. Add margarine. Cook over hot water 20 minutes. Line bottom and sides of greased 2-quart casserole with this mixture. Set aside. Preheat oven to 350° F. Sauté onion, garlic, and green pepper in olive oil until limp and translucent. Pour off excess oil. Add this mixture to beef which has been browned and from which fat drippings have been removed. Then, add tomatoes, corn, and seasonings. Simmer 20 minutes. Spoon into casserole. Cover with olives and grated cheese. Bake 1 hour.

Serves 4

Approximately 151 milligrams of sodium per serving

Low-Sodium Dinner Rolls

1½ cups warm water (about 100° F)
1 package dry yeast
2 tablespoons sugar
6 tablespoons vegetable oil
2 cups whole wheat flour
2 cups enriched white flour
2 teaspoons sesame or poppy seeds

Preheat oven to 375° F. Pour warm water into large mixing bowl; sprinkle with yeast and let stand for 5 minutes. Stir. Add sugar, oil, and whole wheat flour; beat until well blended. Stir in 1 cup white flour to make a soft dough and then knead in remaining 1 cup of white flour. Turn out on floured board and knead for about 10 minutes until smooth and elastic. Place in greased bowl and cover; let rise for about 45 minutes or until doubled in bulk.
Turn out onto floured board and knead a few minutes to remove air pockets. Divide dough in half. Roll each half into

a single long piece and cut into 12 equal slices. Form each slice into a smooth, round ball. Place into two greased 9-inch round cake pans; sprinkle with seeds and cover. Let rise until doubled in bulk, about 30 minutes.

Bake 25 to 30 minutes or until golden brown in color. These freeze well if wrapped air tight.

Makes 24 rolls

Less than 1 milligram of sodium per roll

Herb Margarine

¼ cup unsalted margarine
1 tablespoon fresh lemon juice
1 tablespoon fresh parsley, chopped
1 teaspoon zesty shaker (see recipe)

Soften margarine if not already softened. Add the remaining ingredients and mix until blended well.

This may be used to flavor vegetables or to "top" potatoes.

Approximately 10 milligrams of sodium in this amount of herb margarine

Low-Sodium French Dressing

1 small clove of garlic, crushed
2 tablespoons tarragon vinegar or lemon juice
5 tablespoons salad oil

1 teaspoon sugar
1 teaspoon spicy shaker (see recipe)
¹/₄ teaspoon dry mustard
¹/₈ cup onion, chopped

Whip ingredients together in blender. Refrigerate for at least 4 hours before serving.

Approximately 3 milligrams of sodium per tablespoon

Zingy Vegetable Dip

12 ounces low-sodium tomato juice
¹/₄ cup onion, chopped
¹/₈ cup bell pepper, chopped
1 tablespoon spicy shaker (see recipe)

Whip ingredients together in blender. Best if allowed to chill for at least one hour before serving. Serve with chopped raw vegetables.

Serves 7 (¹/₄ cup per serving)

Approximately 15 milligrams of sodium per serving

Nut Bread

3 cups sifted flour
3¹/₂ teaspoons low-sodium baking powder
³/₄ cup sugar

2 tablespoons soft vegetable shortening
1 egg
1½ cups milk
¾ cup walnuts, chopped

Sift together flour and baking powder and set aside. Mix together thoroughly sugar, shortening, and egg. Stir in milk. Add flour and baking powder to mixture. Blend in chopped nuts. Pour into well-greased 9-inch × 5-inch × 3-inch loaf pan. Let stand 20 minutes before baking. Preheat oven to 350°F (moderate). Bake until wooden pick thrust into center comes out clean. Baking time: 60 to 70 minutes.

Approximately 16 milligrams of sodium per half-inch slice

Apple Brown Betty

2 cups homemade low-sodium bread crumbs
5 tablespoons unsalted butter, melted
3 large apples
½ cup packed light brown sugar
½ teaspoon cinnamon
¼ teaspoon nutmeg
juice of ½ lemon
⅓ cup hot water

Preheat oven to 350°F. Butter 1½-quart baking dish (with lid). Toss crumbs and melted butter together in a bowl. Spread ⅓ of crumb mixture in baking dish. Pare and slice apples in a bowl. Add brown sugar, spices, and lemon juice, gently mixing with apples. Arrange apples and crumbs in layers in baking dish, with a final layer of crumbs on top. Add hot water. Cover baking dish and place in oven. After 20 minutes remove cover and continue baking for additional 20 minutes or until apples are tender. Serve hot with cream.

Serves 4

Approximately 24 milligrams of sodium per serving

Sunshine Cake

1 cup cake flour
1 cup sugar
6 egg whites
½ teaspoon cream of tartar
4 egg yolks, beaten until thick and lemon-colored
½ teaspoon lemon extract

Preheat oven to 300°F. Sift flour and half of sugar together three times. Set aside. Beat egg whites with whisk until foamy, and then add cream of tartar. Continue beating until whisk leaves faint line when drawn across surface of egg whites. Add remaining sugar gradually and continue beating until mixture is very fine and even and egg whites are stiff but not dry. Fold in egg yolks and lemon extract. Sift small amount of the flour and sugar over mixture and fold in carefully, continuing until all flour mixture is used up. Pour into ungreased 10-inch tube pan and bake in slow oven at 300°F for 30 minutes, then increase heat slightly to 325°F and bake 35 minutes longer, or until straw comes out clean. Remove from oven and invert pan on a cake rack until cake is thoroughly cold. Remove from pan and sprinkle lightly with confectioner's sugar, if desired.

Approximately 28 milligrams of sodium in ¹/₁₂ of cake

Apple-Berry Crunch

1 cup homemade low-sodium bread crumbs
2 tablespoons sugar
2 tablespoons unsalted margarine, melted
2 cups applesauce
1 cup blueberries, crushed
8 coconut macaroon cookies, crushed

Preheat oven to 375°F. In bowl, mix together bread crumbs, sugar, and melted margarine. Press crumb mixture on bottom and sides of 1½-quart baking dish. Bake for 8 minutes, until brown. Cool. Then add in layers the following: applesauce, blueberries, and macaroon crumbs, with the final layer the crumbs. Brown topping in 375°F oven. Cool. Serve with whipped cream.

Serves 6

Approximately 51 milligrams of sodium per serving

Lemon Custard Pudding

½ cup sugar
1½ tablespoons unsalted butter

grated rind of 1 lemon
3 eggs, separated
3 level tablespoons flour
1 cup milk
¼ cup lemon juice

Preheat oven to 350°F. Cream sugar, butter, and lemon rind. Beat egg yolks and add to sugar mixture. Stir in flour. Add milk and lemon juice and mix well. Beat egg whites until they form soft peaks. Fold them into batter. Place batter in buttered 1½-quart baking dish. Place baking dish in a pan filled with 1 inch of hot water. Bake 50 to 60 minutes. May be served with heavy cream (which contains 5 milligrams of sodium per tablespoon).

Serves 4

Approximately 76 milligrams of sodium per serving

Baked Pears

4 firm pears
sprinkle of lemon juice
⅓ cup sugar
½ cup water
lemon rind
cinnamon stick

Preheat oven to 300°F. Peel pears, cut in half, and remove cores. Place in ovenware dish and sprinkle with lemon juice. Combine sugar, water, lemon rind and cinnamon stick in saucepan; cook rapidly for 5 minutes. Pour over pears. Bake until pears are tender but still firm. Serve warm or cold, with cream.

Serves 4

Approximately 8 milligrams of sodium per serving, if topped with cream

Raspberry Sauce

2 boxes (10-ounce size) frozen raspberries
2 teaspoons cornstarch
½ cup water
½ cup sugar
1 teaspoon cinnamon
¼ teaspoon cloves

Thaw raspberries, reserving the juice. Mix juice and cornstarch; heat to boiling over medium heat, stirring constantly. Add remaining ingredients and simmer for 10 minutes, stirring frequently. Serve warm.

Serves 5 or 6 (¼ cup per serving)

Approximately 2 milligrams of sodium per serving

Low-Sodium Munchies

¼ cup unsalted margarine
1 tablespoon spicy shaker

2 cups bite-size shredded wheat
1 cup unsalted peanuts
1 cup sunflower seeds

Melt margarine in skillet. Stir in spicy shaker. Add remaining ingredients and toss until well coated with margarine mixture. Cook in skillet, stirring occasionally, for 10 to 15 minutes. Serve warm or cooled. Stores well for several weeks in airtight containers.

Serves 6–8

Approximately 12 milligrams of sodium per serving

Herb Shaker Recipes

If you are accustomed to sprinkling salt on your food at mealtime, try herb shakers instead. Simply mix the ingredients together and place them in a bottle with fairly large holes in the cap; an empty glass spice container may also be used. These herb shakers may be used when dining out or brown bagging. If this is too cumbersome these "spices of life" can be wrapped in plastic and carried in either your pocket or purse.

Savory Shaker
6 teaspoons thyme
3 teaspoons sage
6 teaspoons savory
5 teaspoons rosemary

Trace of sodium per teaspoon

Spicy Shaker

½ teaspoon cayenne
1 tablespoon garlic powder
1 teaspoon onion powder
1 teaspoon black pepper
1 teaspoon basil
1 teaspoon cumin

Approximately 1 milligram of sodium per teaspoon

Zesty Shaker

2 teaspoons onion powder
2 teaspoons paprika
1 teaspoon white pepper
1 teaspoon celery seed
1 teaspoon mace
2 teaspoons dry mustard

Approximately 1 milligram of sodium per teaspoon

Appendix

Sodium Content of Selected Herbs and Spices*

Substance (1 teaspoon, or 1,900 mg.)	Milligrams of Sodium
Allspice	1
Anise seed	trace
Basil	trace
Bay leaf	trace
Caraway seed	trace
Cardamom	trace
Celery seed	3
Chili powder	26
Cinnamon	1
Coriander leaf	1
Coriander seed	1

* SOURCE: John Heinerman, *The Complete Book of Spices: Their Medical, Nutritional and Culinary Uses*, New Canaan, Conn.: Keats Publishing, Inc., 1983.

Substance (1 teaspoon, or 1,900 mg.)	Milligrams of Sodium
Cumin seed	4
Curry powder	1
Dill seed	trace
Dill weed	2
Fennel seed	2
Garlic powder	1
Ginger	1
Horseradish	5
Mace	1
Marjoram	trace
Mustard seed	trace
Nutmeg	trace
Onion powder	1
Oregano	trace
Paprika	1
Parsley	1
Pepper, black	1
Pepper, cayenne	1
Pepper, white	trace
Rosemary	1
Saffron	1
Sage	trace
Savory	trace
Sesame seed	1
Tarragon	1
Thyme	1
Turmeric	1

Bibliography

Altschul, Aaron, and Grommet, Janet K. "Food choices for lowering sodium intake." *Hypertension*, Vol. 4, No. 5, Suppl. III, Sept.–Oct. 1982, pp. 116–120.

Batterson, Mark, and Boddie, W. W., eds. *Salt, the Mysterious Necessity*, The Dow Chemical Co., 1972.

Beard, Trevor C., et al. "Randomized controlled trial of a no-added sodium diet for mild hypertension." *The Lancet*, Aug. 28, 1982, pp. 455–458.

Beretta-Piccoli, C., et al. "Relation of arterial pressure with body sodium, body potassium and plasma potassium in essential hypertension." *Clinical Science*, 63, 1982, pp. 257–270.

Dahl, Lewis K. "Salt and hypertension." *The American Journal of Clinical Nutrition*, Vol. 25, Feb. 1972, pp. 231–244.

Dahl, Lewis K., and Love, R. A. "Evidence for relationship between sodium (chloride) intake and human essential hypertension." *American Medical Association Archives of Internal Medicine*, Vol. 94, 1954, pp. 525–531.

Freis, Edward D. "Salt, volume and prevention of hypertension." *Circulation*, Vol. 53, No. 4, April 1976, pp. 589-595.

Fujita, Toshiro, et al. "Factors influencing blood pressure in salt-sensitive patients with hypertension." *The American Journal of Medicine*, Vol. 69, Sept. 1980, pp. 334–344.

Grim, C. E., et al. "Effects of sodium loading and depletion in normotensive first-degree relatives of essential hypertensives." *Journal Laboratory Clinical Medicine*, Vol. 94, No. 5, Nov. 1979, pp. 764–771.

Heinerman, John. *The Complete Book of Spices: Their Medical, Nutritional and Culinary Uses*. New Canaan, Conn.: Keats Publishing, Inc., 1983.

Hofman, Albert, et al. "A randomized trial of sodium intake and blood pressure in newborn infants." *Journal of the American Medical Association*, Vol. 250, No. 3, July 15, 1983, pp. 370–373.

Kaplan, Norman M. "Renal dysfunction in essential hypertension." *The New England Journal of Medicine*, Vol. 309, No. 17, Oct. 27, 1983, pp. 1052–1053.

Kempner, Walter. "Treatment of hypertensive vascular disease with rice diet." *American Journal of Medicine*, Vol. 4, 1948, pp. 545-577.

Kincaid-Smith, Priscilla. "Malignant hypertension." *Cardiovascular Reviews and Reports*, Vol. 1, No. 1, April 1980, pp. 42–49.

Kolata, Gina. "Value of low-sodium diets questioned." *Science*, Vol. 216, April 2, 1982, pp. 38–39.

Kraus, Barbara. *The Barbara Kraus 1983 Sodium Guide to Brand Names and Basic Foods*. New York: New American Library, 1982.

Lever, A. F., et al. "Sodium and potassium in essential hypertension." *British Medical Journal*, Vol. 283, Aug. 15, 1981, pp. 463–468.

Lindheimer, Marshall, and Katz, Adrian I. "Sodium and diuretics in pregnancy." *The New England Journal of Medicine*, Vol. 288, No. 17, April 26, 1973, pp. 891–894.

Luft, Friedrich C., et al. "Sodium sensitivity and resistance in normotensive humans." *The American Journal of Medicine*, Vol. 72, May 1982, pp. 726–736.

Luft, Friedrich C., and Weinberger, Myron H. "Sodium intake and essential hypertension." *Hypertension*, Vol. 5, No. 4, Sept.–Oct. 1982, Suppl. III, pp. 14–19.

McCarron, David M., et al. "Dietary calcium in human hpertension." *Science*, Vol. 217, July 16, 1982, pp. 267–269.

MacGregor, Graham A., et al. "Double-blind randomized cross-over trial of moderate sodium restriction in essential hypertension." *The Lancet*, Feb. 13, 1982, pp. 351–354.

Marshall, Andrew J. and Barritt, D. W., eds. *The Hypertensive Patient*. Kent, TNI, IXH: Pitman Medical Ltd., and Baltimore, Md.: Univ. Park Press, 1980.

Mendlowitz, Milton. "Sodium and human hypertension." *Clinical and Experimental Hypertension—Theory and Practice*. A 4(3), 1982, pp. 333–340.

Michell, A. R. "Salt appetite, salt intake, and hypertension: A deviation of perspective." *Perspectives in Biology and Medicine*. Spring, 1978, pp. 335–347.

Morgan, T., et al. "Hypertension treated by salt restriction." *The Lancet*, Feb. 4, 1978, pp. 227–230.

Morgan, Trefor, and Myers, John. "Dietary salt and hypertension." *Australian Family Physician*, Vol. 2, No. 4, April 1982, pp. 264–267.

Moser, Marvin, et al., Chm. Joint National Committee on Detection, Evaluation and Treatment of High Blood Pressure. "Report of the Joint National Committee on Detection, Evaluation and Treatment of High Blood Pressure—A Cooperative Study." *Journal of the American Medical Association*, Vol. 237, No. 3, Jan. 17, 1977, pp. 255–261.

Moses, Campbell, ed. *Sodium in Medicine and Health—A Monograph*. Baltimore, Md.: Reese Press, Inc., Salt Institute, 1980.

Office of the Director, National Heart, Lung, and Blood Institute, U.S. Department of Health and Human Services, PHS, NIH. *Hypertension in the USA and USSR: Basic Clinical and Population Research, Second USA-USSR Joint Symposium*, Williamsburg, Va., May 1979, NIH Publ. No. 80–2016, Sept. 1980.

Papper, Solomon, ed. *Sodium: Its Biological Significance*, Boca Raton, Fla.: CRC Press, Inc., 1982.

Pickering, Sir George. "Salt intake and essential hypertension." *Cardiovascular Reviews and Reports*, Vol. 1, No. 1, April 1980, pp. 13–17.

Reisin, E., et al. "Effect of weight loss without salt restriction on the reduction of blood pressure in overweight hypertensive patients." *The New England Journal of Medicine*, Vol. 298, No. 1, Jan. 5, 1978, pp. 1–6.

Report of the Hypertension Task Force, Harriet P. Dustan, Edward D. Frohlich, Chairmen. U.S. Department of Health, Education and Welfare, Public Health Service, National Institutes of Health. NIH Publication No. 79-1623-1631 (Vol. 1–9), Sept. 1979.

Report of the Working Group on Critical Patient Behaviors in the Dietary Management of High Blood Pressure. U.S. Department of Health and Human Services, NIH, Publ. No. 83–2269, Dec. 1982.

Roth, June S. *Salt-free Cooking with Herbs and Spices*. Chicago, Ill.: Henry Regnery Co., 1975.

Symposium on Hypertension and Nutrition. *Annals of Internal Medicine*, May 1983, Vol. 98, No. 5, part 2.

Thomson, William A.R. *Herbs That Heal*. New York: Charles Scribner's Sons, 1976.

Tobian, Louis. "The relationship of salt to hypertension." *The American Journal of Clinical Nutrition*, 32, Dec. 1979, pp. 2739–2748.

Index